16.95

D1599570

To

Bob McCubbin

Antrim is My Stepfather's Name

The Boyhood of Billy the Kid

Jerry Weddle

Foreword by Robert M. Utley

THE ARIZONA HISTORICAL SOCIETY, 1993

Library of Congress Cataloging-in-Publication Data

Weddle, Jerry.
    Antrim is my stepfather's name: the boyhood of Billy the Kid/
Jerry Weddle; foreword by Robert M. Utley.
        p. cm.—(Historical monograph; no. 9)
        Includes bibliographical references and index.
        ISBN 0-910037-31-0
        1. Billy, the Kid—Childhood and youth. 2. Outlaws—Southwest,
New—Biography. 3. Arizona—History—To 1912. 4. Silver City (N.M.)—
Biography. 5. Globe (Ariz.)—Biography. I. Title. II. Series: Historical
monograph (Arizona Historical Society); no. 9.
F786.B54W43 1993
364.1'552'092—dc20
[B]   93-22925
                                                                    CIP

Acknowledgements

The author wishes to thank the following people for their generous assistance: Susan Berry, William M. Bishop, Daniel Buck, Harvel H. Cosper, Dorothy DuBois, Henrietta Lackner DuBois, James Fred DuBois, Jim Essic, Richard C. Fritz, Rosalie Gilliland, Shirley Gustafsen, Pat Humble, Irene F. Kennedy, H. M. Kilburn, Leah Lockart, Robert G. McCubbin, Darlis A. Miller, Betsy Nash, Fred Prevost, Jr., Kathy Quinn, Sally Quinn, Philip J. Rasch, Al Regensberg, Robert L. Spude, Peter L. Steere, Kelly Truesdell, Jean Uhli, and Harvey H. Whitehill III.

List of illustrations

Foreword

by Robert M. Utley

Billy the Kid lives, in the spirit if not in the flesh. Indeed, some believe he lived in the flesh well into the twentieth century, the beneficiary of a conspiracy and cover-up such as has always fascinated Americans. Even for the more sensible, Billy has lost none of his power to stir the imagination. A stream of books, magazines, comic books, folk ballads, motion pictures, and television specials testifies to his continuing public appeal, both in his historical and his legendary guises.

Billy the Kid was a real person, pursuing real adventures on a raw and violent southwestern frontier. He fought bravely and skillfully in the Lincoln County War of 1878 in New Mexico, dabbled in cattle rustling, shot and killed at least four men before scarcely out of his teens, and died in front of a sheriff's six-shooter at the age of twenty-one—truly a short and violent life.

Yet it is not historical reality that shapes the public image of the Kid. Few other figures of the past have inspired such a rash of mythmaking. The Kid most people know is a product of this process, a folk hero encrusted with so many layers of legend as to defy historical inquiry.

Even so, few people, however anonymous, make their way through life without leaving a paper trail for the diligent researcher. Billy was no exception. He presents the historian with formidable challenges, but he is not beyond recapture.

For serious students, the most puzzling period of the Kid's life has been his youth—the years in Silver City, New Mexico, and the Arizona interlude, before he made his more public debut in the Lincoln County War. In the absence of fruitful research, legend has dominated. Now, thanks to a tenacious and level-headed researcher, that period has been filled in.

Jerry Weddle is a true grass-roots historian. He gets on the trail, paper and landscape both, and follows it with the acute sense of an Indian tracking deer through the forest. Where it seems to disappear, he digs beneath the surface and finds evidence invisible to the naked eye. Where others have been content to repeat still others uncritically, Weddle brings a healthy skepticism to supposedly established verities and subjects them to tests of plausibility within the framework of time, place, and culture. He does not abandon the trail until he has run down the quarry.

Here, then, are the missing years in Billy the Kid's life. For those concerned with the Kid of reality, Weddle is to be credited with a signal contribution to history. Perhaps even those most afflicted by legend will find, as is frequently true, that fact is not only stranger than fiction, but more compelling as well.

Introduction

Who was Billy the Kid? It seems that a life so deeply entrenched in the lore of the land should be substantially documented. When I began my research, I found only his violence written up. Gunfights and acts of derring-do preoccupied the early journalists and entertained the reading public. Printers spilled a lot of ink on the twenty-one men he supposedly killed—according to legend, one man for each year of his life. As a result, violence is largely what survives in the evidence and in the literature.

This raises the question of the character of the person who committed the violence. Book after book portrays Billy as a wanton killer from beginning to end, his life nothing more than a grim series of uninterrupted shootings. In the history books, Billy remains unaffected by the momentous events in which he participates. There is no development of personality, no progression from birth to death, no explanation of motive or intent, and no effort made to place him within the context of a frontier society. Judiciously used, eyewitness accounts provide a biographer with the means to find the human dimension in a life that has been distorted or lost to the passage of time.

There are some remarkable firsthand accounts by those who met Billy before, during, and after the Lincoln County War. Contrary to popular belief, factional bias does not rule out the many insights oldtimers had to offer. This is especially true of Louis Abraham, Mary Richards, Charley Stevens, Chauncey Truesdell, and others who neither lived in Lincoln County nor fought in the war. Without their testimony, the biographer is left with an artifact instead of a person. Indeed, some influential historians prefer an artifactual Billy and scoff at applying the same biographical methods that they routinely apply to other historic figures.

Eyewitness accounts were largely concerned with matters not ordinarily associated with Billy the Kid: namely, a preoccupation with the things of childhood, the daily struggle of frontier life, the burgeoning of law enforcement, the economic and political upheavals of the time. A more comprehensive study of Billy's life and times convinced me that the literature displayed an ignorance of these fundamental matters, which, after all, must have shaped him. I thought that an investigation into his formative years, a largely unknown period between 1873 and 1877, might unearth some semblance of an authentic Billy.

I found that Billy's contemporaries in Silver City had to reach back into their own childhood to remember someone they knew for only a few years. If their accounts are vague and somewhat confused, it is due to the erosion of memory rather than a conscious effort to deceive. For instance, interviewers never pressed oldtimers who insisted that Billy was a victim of circumstances to explain just what those circumstances were. The recurrence of similar if somewhat tenuous threads makes their accounts coherent. Similar, because Louis Abraham and Emma and Harry Whitehill, among others, remembered going to school with Billy; tenuous, because historians never followed up on it. Billy's contemporaries remembered family and friends, getting into mischief, putting on minstrel shows, holding foot races, working for wages and room and board, and all the ordinary things youngsters do. But historians, always at odds with the oldtimer, concentrated instead on Billy's alleged killings and ignored everything else. It is not that Billy's contemporaries mis-remembered, but that historians missed the richer story they wanted to tell.

It should come as no surprise when public records corroborate and enhance eyewitness accounts. For example, the local paper mentioned the foot races that Harry Whitehill described. One can trace the minstrel shows in which he and Billy performed in the same way. And the matter-of-fact accounts by Miles L. Wood remain the best evidence for following Billy's trail through Arizona. Used as a sounding board for additional research, hitherto unrelated evidence became relevant, and contradictory evidence clarified. Where eyewitness testimony and documentation converge, we arrive at historical fact.

I want to offer Billy the Kid enthusiasts an interpretation based on those facts, instead of on the myriad false assumptions that make up the literature. For instance, contrary to popular belief, there is no reason to believe, and no evidence to prove, that he beheaded a kitten with a jackknife. This lurid fiction gains credence through repetition, but that does not make it true. My method of avoiding the pitfall was to re-evaluate the original source material. And the only valid way to characterize Billy is to rely on the observations of those who lived within his sphere; not to defend his larceny or violence but, like Louis Abraham, Gus Gildea, and Clara Truesdell, to understand it within the context of the life he experienced.

Even before the twentieth century, Billy the Kid had grown into a pervasive myth. And like any other myth, Billy the Kid is a chameleon who changes appearance with each succeeding story. We have lost the authentic Billy, the boy who grew up on a harsh frontier in which many people found his actions more ennobling than criminal. No one made a real effort to record the facts when they were still retrievable. No one knew what questions to ask when the people who knew the answers were still living. No one tried to reconcile the difference between a hostile press, politically motivated by the Lincoln County War, with the warmer perceptions of those who actually knew him. Out of the dichotomy grew the myth of Billy the Kid. Mythmaking thrives where fact is scarce, and, as a result, only a skeletal reconstruction of the boyhood of Billy the Kid is possible.

Jerry Weddle

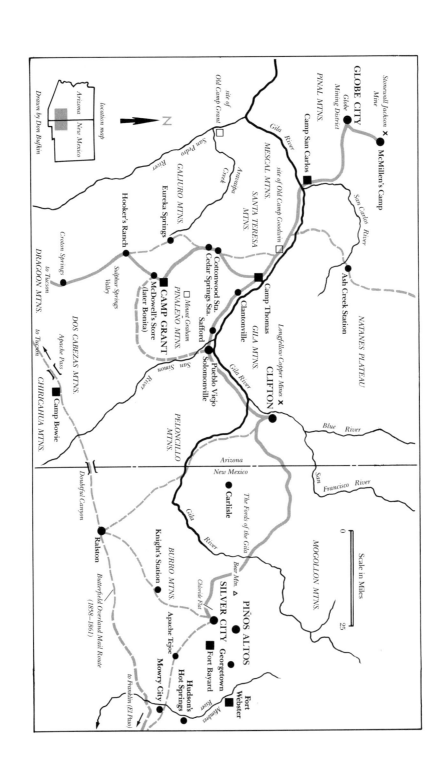

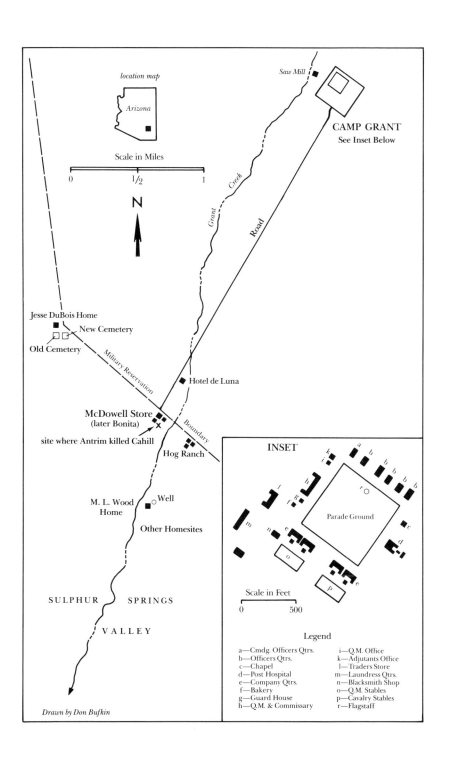

location map

Arizona

Scale in Miles

0   1/2   1

N

Grant *Creek*

Road

Saw Mill

CAMP GRANT
See Inset Below

Jesse DuBois Home

New Cemetery

Old Cemetery

Military Reservation

Hotel de Luna

McDowell Store
(later Bonita)

site where Antrim killed Cahill

Boundary

Hog Ranch

M. L. Wood
Home

Well

Other Homesites

SULPHUR   SPRINGS

V A L L E Y

Drawn by Don Bufkin

INSET

Parade Ground

Scale in Feet

0   500

Legend

a—Cmdg. Officers Qtrs.
b—Officers Qtrs.
c—Chapel
d—Post Hospital
e—Company Qtrs.
f—Bakery
g—Guard House
h—Q.M. & Commissary

i—Q.M. Office
k—Adjutants Office
l—Traders Store
m—Laundress Qtrs.
n—Blacksmith Shop
o—Q.M. Stables
p—Cavalry Stables
r—Flagstaff

Billy the Kid first comes into focus in 1873 as William Henry McCarty, one of many children growing up wild in the streets of Silver City, New Mexico Territory. Born and raised in southern Indiana, he spent his early childhood with his widowed mother, Catherine McCarty, and his younger brother, Joseph Bonney McCarty. When Catherine learned that she had tuberculosis, doctors advised her to move west. The McCartys pulled up stakes and moved to Wichita, Kansas. William Henry Harrison Antrim, a son of a close-knit Irish clan from the nearby town of Anderson and a long-time acquaintance of Catherine's, probably helped them. But after two years, her health suddenly took a turn for the worse. Everyone hoped that a move to a climate high and dry would save her life. The plan also suited her friend and neighbor William Antrim, who, struck with his own ailment, gold fever, wanted to seek his fortune in the mountains of southwestern New Mexico.[1]

Antrim brought the family to a brief stay in Denver, then on to Santa Fe, New Mexico. For some months they lived with his sister, Mary Antrim Hollinger. Catherine's health must have improved in the high, thin air, for on March 1, 1873, she married William Antrim in the First

Presbyterian Church. The Reverend D. F. McFarland performed the ceremony, with Mrs. McFarland, their daughter Katie, and the bride's two sons as witnesses. The Antrims moved into the Exchange Hotel, where young Billy may have worked as an energetic messenger.[2]

As a result of the marriage, the family now contained two William Henrys. To avoid confusing the boy with the man, Catherine started calling Billy by his middle name, Henry. The youth had always answered to Billy McCarty, and he never quite grew accustomed to being called Henry Antrim. His contemporaries knew and called him by both names.[3]

Soon after the wedding, the new family traveled down the Rio Grande and turned west into Grant County. The spectacular mineral discoveries in this section of the Continental Divide had become national news and enticed William Antrim. The region was the native home of hostile Apaches, who murdered and plundered along the roads and trails that connected the mining camps and towns with Fort Bayard. Two companies of the Eighth Cavalry and two companies of the Fifteenth Infantry patrolled the copper hills and silver fields, offering some small protection to prospectors.

Into this environment came William Antrim with his ailing bride and two stepsons. At first they settled in Georgetown, a rough and ready mining camp just beginning to form into a town. Resident Ed Moulton, a young sawmill operator and saloonkeeper, befriended them. But Catherine wanted to raise her sons in a more stable community, so their stay in Georgetown was brief. Much to Antrim's annoyance, they moved southeast to Silver City.[4]

When they arrived in late March or early April of 1873, Silver City was one mining town that had already "passed the point of beans straight," as one newspaper described it.

William Antrim (center).

Unlike any other town in the territory, it was a well-structured and surprisingly progressive community. Silver City spread across a broad valley on the downslope between two hillsides. It resembled an eastern city, with streets plotted into a dozen rectangular blocks. Two-story edifices built out of red brick stood next to sun-baked adobes and weathered log cabins. A variety of mercantile and service stores testified to the town's success. Stagecoaches, freight wagons, and prairie schooners rolled through the tree-lined streets. Stamp mills south of town made thunder pulverizing ore from as far away as Arizona and old Mexico. Dynamite blasts reverberated in the surrounding mountains.[5]

Antrim deposited his new family in a sturdy log cabin on south Main Street, in the southwest corner of the block at the intersection of Broadway. John Swisshelm, one of the town's founders, had probably built it as one of the first cabins during the beans-straight days. The structure was so small the Antrims could not swing a cat in it, but they were lucky to find a new home before the next tide of immi-

Photo purported to be Catherine McCarty Antrim.

grants swelled the population from 900 to more than 2,000 residents. The surge in population created a shortage of drinking water and housing so severe that the local barber, P. Wagner, had to stop selling baths and turn his fenced yard into a campground for newcomers living in tents.[6]

Stepping out of the front door of her cabin, Catherine glanced across the street at I. N. Cohen & Co.'s drygoods store and Billy Sidow's butcher shop. To the right, looking north up Main, an old adobe stood in near ruins at the other end of the block, opposite the Keystone Hotel, and right beyond it, McGary's bowling alley and dance hall. To the left, looking across the intersection of Broadway, the business district lined up along south Main. On the east side stood Gideon Truesdell's merchandise store, Matt Derbyshire's News Depot and furniture store, H. M. Porter's General Merchandise Store, and a couple of saloons. Looking diagonally across the intersection, to the west side of Main, stood Dr. G. W. Bailey's apothecary and post office, J. B. Morrill's store, and couple of saloons. Main Street

Silver City in 1872.

curled southward into the Cienega, where the chimneys of several smelting furnaces poured an acrid smoke into the sky twenty-four hours a day. The smoke canopied the lower half of town, and Catherine inhaled it into her slowly failing lungs.

The next blocks over were Bullard and Texas streets, lined with goods and service stores as well as residences. Walking out of the rear of the cabin, Catherine looked south down Hudson Street and saw the Elephant Corral; the Star Hotel, with its ten rooms and long bar; Colonel Richard Hudson's Legal Tender Livery & Feed Stable; and a couple of saloons. Opposite the cabin's back door stood J. B. Bennett's Mercantile Store, and north up Hudson, Catherine viewed the county jail and a growing number of red-light saloons.[7]

Like other men in Silver City, William Antrim gambled heavily and set out to learn the rudiments of mining. He had an income from properties rented in Wichita, and found work as a carpenter and as a butcher in Richard Knight's meat market, but he mostly gambled. It is doubtful that he did much to support his family. As they settled in, Antrim made long and frequent trips to Chloride Flat, Georgetown, Pinos Altos, and the Carlisle mines near the Arizona border.[8]

Catherine took in boarders for an income. During the housing shortage, travelers could find shelter in private homes for a nominal fee. The town followed this practice to encourage the tide of immigrants to stay, but Catherine did it because she had to. Ed Moulton, her husband's friend from Georgetown, was an overnight guest in the small cabin from time to time. Catherine also baked pies and "sweetcakes" that sold easily to townsfolk.

She left a lasting impression on the neighborhood boys who came to play with her sons, especially thirteen-year-old Louis Abraham. A half-century later, he vividly remembered the Antrim household as "an ordinary good American home. Good parents, and a good environment in the home." Catherine, whom he called "as good as she could be," drew him to her hearth. She "always welcomed the boys with a smile and a joke. The cookie jar was never empty to the boys. From school each afternoon we made straight for the Antrim home to play," said Louis. "My mother was dead, and my father had a Spanish woman for a cook, her food never tasted as good as the meals that Mrs. Antrim cooked. I ate many meals in the home of Billie the Kid and I know that I was welcome."[9]

At first, Catherine's health seemed to be improving. She and Billy, her older son, enthusiastically joined in the town's *bailes* (dances), held every Monday, Wednesday, Saturday, and Sunday night in dance halls that were usually part of a saloon. One establishment, McGary's Hall on north Main, doubled as the first church and the first courthouse. In Ward's Hall, only men entered by the front door and walked past the gaming tables. In the middle stretched the bar, and in the back was the dance floor, 200 feet long and 50 feet wide. Double barn doors opened onto the alley, where ladies made their entrance. Local custom forbid them to come in through the saloon. A dance cost four bits—25 cents to the lady and 25 cents to the bar. "Each dance did not last long," wrote Dan Rose, a friend of Billy's, "just long enough to get acquainted." The townspeople turned out in droves to twirl until daylight. Louis Abraham was there, too, watching the "jolly Irish lady, full of life, and her fun and mischief. Mrs. Antrim could dance the Highland Fling as well as the best of the dancers."[10]

Catherine's sons quickly met Louis and the other boys in town. Being in the minority in Silver City, the Anglo youths stayed together, congregating at the Antrims' house every day after school. In addition to Louis and his brother Hyman, the gathering included Cortie Bennett, Anthony Conner, Jr., and four sets of brothers: John and Vincent Mays, Gideon and Chauncey Truesdell, Albert and Charley Stevens, and their cousins Harry and Wayne Whitehill, among others. By 1875, Daniel and Thomas Rose joined the fold. At Catherine's hearth, the boys played marbles, held foot races, wrestled, and made like pirates.[11]

William Henry McCarty was about twelve years old when he arrived in Silver City, although he looked younger. His friends thought he was small for his age, almost diminutive. His slender build, delicate hands, small feet, and soft, high voice gave ten-year-old Anthony Conner the impression that "he was undersized, and really girlish looking. I don't think he weighed over 75 pounds." There was no doubt in Anthony's mind that in 1873, "Billy was about twelve years old."

"Henry was only a small boy," agreed ten-year-old Chauncey Truesdell, "small for his age and kind of skinny." Yet another observer commented, "He was a mild man-

Louis Abraham.

nered, flaxen-haired, blue-eyed boy." By contrast, younger brother Joseph Bonney McCarty, or Joe Antrim, was "larger and very husky," said Chauncey. "He looked to be a year and a half or two older than Henry."[12]

Young Billy liked to dress well, and everyone noticed his neat appearance and clean habits. He was unfailingly courteous, especially to the ladies. Like his mother, he was a spirited singer and dancer. He had an alert mind and could come up with a snappy proverb for every occasion. He read well and wrote better than most adults. A taste for sweets resulted in bad teeth, and two of his upper incisors protruded slightly. His rambunctious sense of humor always got a laugh, whether it be on himself or someone else. Because of his small stature, he took a lot of ribbing from those bigger and stronger, but what he lacked in size he made up with tremendous energy and quick reflexes. Anxious to please, eager to impress, willing to take extraordinary risks, Billy would dare anything to prove his worth. The other schoolkids soon realized that he had genuine courage.[13]

Charley Stevens.

Billy and his compadres cut quite a swath through Silver City. O. L. Scott, the articulate and somewhat grumpy editor of the town's leading paper, *Mining Life*, named the group of youngsters "the Village Arabs," contemporary slang for boys inhabiting the streets. "In the race of life," he pontificated, "we know of a few boys in town who would benefit by coming in on the home stretch across the maternal knee." As early as May of 1873, he editorialized that the street urchins deserved all the advantages of "a real American education," and he lobbied to build a public school. "Our children are growing up in idleness without an opportunity to improve their minds," he complained. Scott never stated just what the Village Arabs did to prompt such urgency, but by August, he equated the need for a public school with the need for a secure jail.[14]

The town had a limited treasury and could afford just one facility. The town council voted to spend the money on the top priority—the jail. The residents' taxes would pay for the public school, making it free to pupils between the

Chauncey Truesdell.

ages of five and fifteen years. Few people could afford the private school, which Jessie Anderson taught in Robert Black's house. To raise the funds, the men on the town council formed the school commission, pending the governor's approval of their posts. In the meantime, the women of Silver City formed the Ladies Educational Society and galvanized the citizenry. They held dances, dinners, and other social functions to raise $2,500 to build a schoolhouse. According to Black's design, it was to be red brick, twenty by forty feet, one story high. The front would have a double door and a window on each side, with three windows each on the other three sides. By mid-October, the Ladies Educational Society had raised $169.50.[15]

Progressive though it may have been, Silver City was still a frontier mining town, and the brothers Antrim could not avoid its lawless element. Whatever they and the Village Arabs were doing to cause concern, their worst behavior was child's play compared to that of their elders. There were a dozen shootings in July and August of 1873, and the violence continued through the fall. "Lawlessness has been on the rampage," complained editor Scott. David Abraham, a well-to-do merchant and father of Louis, killed his third man with a shotgun that year.

The town's most elaborate saloon, the Orleans Club on Main Street, contributed significantly to the many drunken brawls that disrupted the harmony of Silver City's streets. The most memorable altercation occurred on August 6, a Wednesday night, when owner Joe Dyer assaulted William Wilson in one of the clubrooms. Wilson overpowered Dyer and slashed his face and abdomen with a penknife. Authorities arrested Wilson, examined him, and discharged him on a plea of self-defense. Dyer recovered, though he was scarred for life. Later pulp writers attributed the crime to Billy the Kid.[16]

Daily life in Silver City went on despite the crime rate, including educating the younger populace. Billy and Joe were among the kids enumerated in November 1873 to find out how many children between five and fifteen years old lived in town. Out of 826 inhabitants of Silver City, there were 30 Anglo and 119 Mexican potential pupils. The statistic so impressed the school commissioners that in January of 1874, they finally organized a public school. Still lacking the funds to build, they rented McGary's Hall on north Main Street and secured the services of Dr. J. Webster, the first of many teachers who yielded to the wear and tear of the Village Arabs.

The Antrim boys were two of the thirty pupils in attendance through the semester, which lasted from January 5 to March 28, 1874. Among the students were Cortie Bennett, Carrie Bertchy, James and Mary Davis, Alice Dyer, Roscoe Ginn, Richard Justice, Lily Lefer, Charles and Al Rosencranz, Charley and Al Stevens, Gideon and Chauncey Truesdell, and the Whitehills.[17]

Some of his classmates remembered Henry Antrim. "I went to school with Billy the Kid," said Louis Abraham.

"[I] went to school with Billie Antrim," said Charley Stevens, fourteen at the time.

"My sister and I went to school with Billy," said Harry Whitehill.[18]

Each evening, after classes, about a dozen of the Village Arabs prepared a race course on Market Street, near the office of *Mining Life*. Their antics attracted the attention of passersby, and editor Scott, who never missed a thing in his columns, commented that the races "are carried on throughout with great hilarity and scarcely a difference." Emma Whitehill remembered that "my brother and I played with Billie the Kid." Harry described the recreation:

> The boys . . . would have someone be their race horse and would bet just for fun. I was Louie Abraham's race horse. Everytime before a race Louie would come around with a bottle . . . I dont know what it was . . . and say, "Lift up your feet." So I would lift up my feet and Louie would put some of the stuff out of the bottle on it. Of course, there wasn't anything to it, and it couldn't help me to win, but I always imagined that it would make me win and I could outrun anyone in Silver City until I was 21 years old.[19]

Still, the mischief continued. On February 4, a Wednesday night, butcher Richard Knight turned his back just long enough for someone to snatch $35 out of the money drawer. "It will pay to keep a good look-out for these petty thieves now," advised O. L. Scott. "There are a number of them in town and they don't let any chances slip." On March 28, the day classes ended, one of Scott's correspondents suggested that amateur theatricals would keep youngsters occupied and, at the same time, raise money for the schoolhouse. He suggested moral plays, such as T. S. Arthur's *Ten Nights in a Barroom* and Harriet Beecher Stowe's

Uncle Tom's Cabin. Thus Silver City began the honored tradition of minstrel shows, held in the meeting and dance halls. They began as ragtag improvisations but eventually developed into full-scale theatrical productions.[20]

The plays did not always go smoothly. Harry Whitehill remembered how a disputed bet could ruin a minstrel show:

> I was what you call the property man. Well, some of us boys were walking down to Bailey's Drug Store on the other side of the old saloon. Billy the Kid was right behind me. He gave me a shove and I turned around and cussed him; and Billy gave me another shove and I went down in the flood. Well, I would have been drowned right there if two men hadn't come out of the Post Office just then and saved me.
>
> That night we went over there to give the minstrel. Billy was the Head Man in the show. When he came around to me I said "I want you to pay me what you owe me." And Billy said that he wasn't going to. "Well, if you don't I am going to tear this show up," I said. But Billy wouldn't give me a thing, so I went through a curtain and pulled it after me, you know. Later I happened to meet him but [Charley] Stevens kept him from beating me up.[21]

Mischief-making aside, it may truthfully be said that Billy McCarty, the Village Arabs' leading minstrel, helped raise the money to build the first organized public-school system in New Mexico.

No sooner had O. L. Scott announced that the new jail was ready (Patrick Shanley's wagon train had delivered the iron for a door and window bars in January) than the Village Arabs again aroused his ire. Late on the night of March 11, a Wednesday, some of the boys broke through a window in a dance hall, shattering the oil lamps and chimneys on a table under the window as they tumbled through. The hall gave them access to the adjoining Bank Exchange Saloon. They took a lot of coins from the till and carried off several buckets of whiskey. No one ever identified the culprits, but the heist foreshadowed Billy's grandiose money-making schemes.

Scott was indignant. "These thefts are getting to be too common, and are perpetrated by a lot of youngsters who infest the town ekeing [*sic*] out an existence and making themselves obnoxious to the people by just such depredations," he editorialized. Scott suggested that the unnamed youths spend their nights in the new jail, "while their muscle might be utilized on our streets during the day."[22]

In the spring of 1874, Ash Upson, a newspaperman, found shelter in the Antrim cabin while prospecting in the area. The inebriated Pecos Valley schoolteacher sent exaggerated stories of the Wild West to eastern newspapers. Later he played a decisive role in transforming William Henry McCarty into the mythical Billy the Kid. With his usual flair for overstatement, he wrote of Catherine, "many a hungry 'tenderfoot' has had cause to bless the fortune that led him to her door." He described his proprietress:

> She was evidently of Irish descent. . . . She was about the medium height, straight, and graceful in form, with regular features, light blue eyes, and luxuriant golden hair. She was not a beauty, but what the world calls a fine-looking woman. She kept boarders in Silver City, and her charity and goodness of heart were proverbial. . . . In all her deportment she exhibited the unmistakable characteristics of a lady—a lady by instinct and education.[23]

In fact, Catherine's condition was deteriorating. Charley Stevens witnessed her decline and introduced her to his elder sister, Mary Stevens Hudson. Mary and her husband, Richard Hudson, owned Hudson's Hot Springs twenty-six miles southeast of town. People thought that the sulphur baths were a miraculous healer, and patients with all kinds of ailments kept the hotel thriving. Mary brought Catherine to the springs and took a personal interest in her

David Abraham,
father of Louis.

treatments. They became friends. "She was a sweet gentle little lady," Mary recalled, "as fond of her sons as any mother should be." The sulphur baths failed to restore her lungs, and by the first of May, Catherine was confined to her bed in the cabin on Main Street. As the struggle to breathe intensified, Catherine realized that her days of dancing the Highland Fling were over.[24]

Clara Louisa Truesdell, Chauncey's mother, had graduated from a Chicago nursing school, and she cared for Catherine during the next four months. Antrim was gone on one of his trips, and Catherine must have felt—not without reason—that he had abandoned them. Her main concern during this time was the welfare of her sons. She mistrusted her husband to raise them, and Billy had begun to get into trouble. "When Mrs. Antrim was sick, she was worried about Joe and Henry," explained Chauncey, "and she made my mother promise to look out for them if anything should happen to her."[25]

As their mother's illness worsened, Billy and Joe kept up

Clara Louisa Truesdell.

their schooling. On Monday, May 18, a new teacher, Mrs. Pratt, began a summer-school session, a week late in order to finish repairs on the school's roof. The commissioners had renovated a dilapidated adobe on Main Street, at the other end of the block from the Antrim cabin. They put the pupils, including Billy and Joe, to work sweeping out the floor, taking down a partition, and whitewashing the walls. Robert Black, the building contractor, built and donated desks and chairs. Mrs. Pratt spent an arduous summer teaching the Village Arabs before heavy August rains turned the layer of dirt on the roof into a pool of mud. The load spilled through onto the heads of the pupils, and Mrs. Pratt dismissed school a week early, never to return.[26]

The bedridden Catherine could not prevent Billy from trying to goad Charley Stevens into robbing Matt Derbyshire's store. Derbyshire sold mainly furniture, but he also had a candy stand and a busy news depot, where Billy bought dime novels whenever he had a dime. The boys frequented the shop, and the owner had taken a liking to them. The last week of May 1874, Derbyshire was also selling tickets to a traveling Mexican circus that had come to town. "The boys, old and young, have had a good time," wrote editor Scott, "the younger portion by following the clown and band through the streets in their daily promenade, and the larger ones by applauding the tightrope and trapeze performers when they made a failure."

In his window, Derbyshire displayed costume jewelry that the circus would raffle off. Huddled in the alley behind the store, Billy and Charley planned to break in, steal the jewelry, and make tracks for old Mexico to dispose of it. "He was a schemer," blamed Charley, "always trying to figure out some way of putting something over to get money."

On the eve of the burglary, Charley weakened and told his father, Isaac J. Stevens, who took him by the hand to confess to Matt Derbyshire. When the grownups asked the boy who had inveigled him into such a ridiculous scheme, Charley admitted, "the Kid had me hypnotized." The men agreed to spare him further humiliation by withholding the true source of their information from Billy. They called both boys on the carpet and gave them a stern scolding. When Billy asked how they found out, the men told him an old drunk had been sleeping outside, overheard their plans, and reported it. The explanation seemed to satisfy the boy. Perhaps this was the incident that so angered Catherine that she warned her son, "you'll hang before you're 21" if he did not mend his ways.[27]

Catherine McCarty Antrim, age forty-five, died on Wednesday, September 16, 1874, after four months in bed, wheezing and gasping for air. Her husband was absent. "When she was dying she said she was leaving two boys in a wild country," said Chauncey Truesdell, "and asked my mother if she would try to help them." Clara promised to look after the boys. The Stevenses, the Truesdells, and the

Whitehills were among the mourners at the funeral service, held at 2 o'clock Thursday afternoon in the Antrim cabin. In William Antrim's absence, Louis Abraham helped to dig the grave. His father, David Abraham, transported Catherine's body in his surrey several blocks to the cemetery. "Billie and I . . . ," remembered Louis, "soon learned we had lost a dear ally and friend." While Catherine lived, the boys were on their best behavior. Her death indeed proved catastrophic to Billy and Joe.[28]

Their stepfather, William Antrim, was a mild-mannered, indifferent man. He understood how to do a day's work but not how to raise someone else's children. Nor was he inclined to spend his hard-earned money supporting them—"some people say he kept the first dime he ever made," said Agnes Meador Snider, his landlady in later years. His desultory care was largely responsible for the trouble the boys had been getting into.[29]

Now, with Catherine gone, he moved the boys out of the cabin and into the home of Richard Knight, the butcher, and his wife, Sara. Antrim worked at Knight's shop. Sara's kid brother, Anthony Conner, Jr., was a companion of Billy's. Anthony recalled:

> We were just boys together. I never remember Billy doing anything out of the way, anymore than the rest of us. Billy got to be quite a reader. He would scarcely have his dishes washed, until he would be sprawled out somewhere reading a book. It was the same down at the butcher shop, if he was helping around there. The first thing you would know, he would be reading. Finally he took to reading the *Police Gazette* and dime novels.[30]

By the end of 1874, William Antrim was ready for a change. He arranged for thirteen-year-old Billy to live with Chauncey's parents, Gerald and Clara Truesdell. They had just bought the Star Hotel on Hudson Street, renovated it,

18

and renamed it the Exchange Hotel. The boy would wait on tables and clean up to pay for his room and board.

Antrim sent young Joseph to live with the family of Joe Dyer, proprietor of the Orleans Club, and work in the saloon for his keep. There the youth grew up gambling, serving liquor, placing bets, running numbers, and delivering messages. Within a few years, Joe was thoroughly immersed in the unbridled atmosphere. "We used to have a pretty good sized Chinatown in Silver City and there were several opium dens running then," remembered Olive Whitehill, Wayne's sister. "Wayne said he and some other boys used to go there and peek through the cracks in the windows and doors to see who was smoking opium. Wayne told me that they saw Billy the Kid's brother, Joe, down there smoking opium, along with the Chinamen. At least I never heard tell of Billy doing that." Antrim came and went freely, pursuing opportunities while leaving his irrepressible stepsons to fend for themselves. He apparently felt that he had discharged his parental responsibility.[31]

Despite their hardships, the orphaned boys continued their education. On Monday, September 14, 1874, just two days before Catherine died, the fall school semester had begun. The new teacher was Mary P. Richards, an elegant twenty-five-year-old woman educated in England. O. L. Scott looked in on her class and found that her twenty-nine pupils "had their interest excited and their advancement was certain."[32]

Richards certainly piqued Billy's interest, and a mutual affection sprang up between teacher and pupil. Years later the schoolteacher told her daughter that her student "was a scrawny little fellow with delicate hands and an artistic nature . . . always quite willing to help with the chores around the school-house." She found him "no more of a problem in school than any other boy growing up in a min-

Whitehill family: (back row from left) Hattie, Harry, Con, Emma, (front) Wayne, Ollie, Josie.

ing camp." Billy noticed that his teacher was ambidextrous, and so was he; surely, he thought, they must be related.[33]

In October, a new after-school diversion kept the Village Arabs from the straight and narrow. Charlie Sun, a Chinese immigrant, arrived to open his hand laundry on north Bullard Street. He had found Albuquerque tough going. His presence in Silver City alarmed Nellie Johnson, the town laundress who lived across the street from the *Mining Life*. She advertised: "Boys, that Chinaman can't do as well for you as I can; bring your washing to Texas Street."[34]

The boys soon learned that their parents and O. L. Scott would look the other way when it came to harassing Charlie Sun. "Because of the amusing sing-song vocabulary of the Chinaman, his laundry became quite a rendezvous for all the mischievous boys of the town," said Charley Stevens, "and he was the target of their jokes." "We didn't want any Chinamen there," added Wayne Whitehill. "We just wanted to chase all the Chinamen out of the town." Several years later, journalists angered the town's residents when they

Anthony Conner, Jr., right, and his fraternal twin, Elijah, in 1880, a month short of their seventeenth birthday.

wrote that Billy began his fabled career of crime by killing a Chinese laundryman in Silver City.

All of his friends and acquaintances denied it. "Billy never killed anyone in Silver City," insisted Louis Abraham.

"The story about his killing a man here in Silver City is all foolishness," said Anthony Conner.

"The Kid never killed anyone in Silver City," agreed Charley Stevens, who would not have missed it if he had.

"That's all poppycock," concurred Wayne Whitehill.[35]

Billy was still a schoolboy, not yet an outlaw. He and Joe continued their schooling, and O. L. Scott continued to observe their teacher. He praised Mary Richards for turning rambunctious kids into attentive scholars. At the school Christmas party, all the pupils excelled at recitation. Robert Black, the contractor, rewarded them with Christmas gifts. So ended Billy's third semester in public school. One can only speculate on the subject of his recitation.

His fourth semester began the following year, on Monday, January 18, 1875. Emma Whitehill and Daniel and

Thomas Rose joined the class that winter. This time Scott complained:

> The larger boys, we are sorry to see, were inattentive. It is a shame for the big lubberly boys to lean against each other, or to hang their bodies while in recitation class . . . the number in attendance was, perhaps, half of what should be there, but we do not wonder children should dislike to attend school in such a tumbledown affair . . . when will the children have the pleasure of assembling in a pleasant, clean, well-lighted and ventilated room?[36]

During the summer of 1875, while Billy attended Mary Richards's class, domestic problems in the Truesdell family compelled him to leave. While keeping close ties with Clara and Chauncey, he found lodging in the home of a Mrs. Brown. To pay his way, he worked at odd jobs for various merchants. At Knight's butcher shop and later for his competitor, the City Meat Market owned by Charles Bottom, the youth killed steers, skinned and gutted the carcasses, and chopped them into meat. Once, when Bottom was sick, Billy persuaded his boss to let him ride the butcher's "fine racing mare" through hazardous Indian country to retrieve medicinal cherry bark, thought to relieve fevers and chills. Billy, aboard the swift horse, made the twenty-eight-mile round trip in a day, returning with the bark and demonstrating to Bottom that he had "plenty of nerve."[37]

Billy increasingly took to gambling for an income. Residents of the frontier accepted it as a way of earning a living, and the men of Silver City gambled on everything from dogfights to the weather. Like his stepfather and his brother, Billy worked diligently at cards. In the Orleans Club and other saloons, he quickly realized that men thought a boy would be easy pickings, and they trusted him to deal poker and monte, the most popular games. "He became a very fine card player," remembered Charley Stevens, "and had picked up many card sharp tricks."

Also, Billy probably pumped the bellows for blacksmith Levi Miller. The shop of "the Village Blacksmith," as his sign said, was known as a hangout for the idle class. Miller and his rough friends found the boy's slight build and easy ways so amusing that they made him an object of derision. One time Margaret Keays Miller, who brought her husband's lunch every day at noon, overheard their invectives and sent the boy home. "Stop it," she told her husband, "you are making him mean." Despite his wife's warning, Miller apparently provoked the boy into a violent rage. Billy's friends dissuaded him from trying to shoot the blacksmith with an old muzzleloader shotgun.

Whatever actually happened, "the story of Billie the Kid killing a blacksmith in Silver City is false," insisted Louis Abraham.

"All those stories about him killing various persons here in Grant County are false," agreed Anthony Conner. "There isn't a bit of truth in any of them."

"Not hardly," said Dick Clark, a citizen of Silver City.

"They write so many lies about the boy," retorted Ed Moulton to Jim Blair, his son-in-law, "and I know the ones are false about his killings in Grant County."[38]

But as Charles Bottom and others observed, Billy possessed a good deal of nerve. He exhibited "a proclivity for breaking the Eighth Commandment" in the eyes of the new sheriff, Harvey H. Whitehill. In April of 1875, the town council voted Whitehill, then the county coroner, into the sheriff's office. (His predecessor, Sheriff Charles McIntosh, wounded in the line of duty and disgusted with the job, the lack of pay, and the unsupportive citizenry, had absconded with the county funds.) Sheriff Whitehill was a huge, powerfully built man with a deep voice and a kindly disposition, the father of Billy's friends Emma, Harry, and Wayne. Soon after Whitehill assumed office, Billy committed "his first offense . . . the theft of several pounds of butter from a ranchman by the name of [Abel L.] Webb, living near Silver City, and which he disposed of to one of the local merchants," remembered the lawman. "His guilt was easily established, but upon promise of good behavior, he was released."[39]

Though a minor incident, the theft illustrated that Billy's schemes for making money were becoming more desperate. Friends observed how poverty pulled him deeper into larceny. He was "a little mischievous at times," admitted Louis Abraham, more "than the rest of us with a little more nerve."

"Billie the Kid was not a bad boy in his school days," said Dick Clark. "The Kid, like other boys, was full of fun and deviltry."

"Billy was one of the best boys in town," stated Anthony Conner, who added cryptically, "I know he was a better boy than I was."

"The boy was an ordinary boy," said a resident of Silver City, "though he began to get into trouble at an early age."[40]

His second brush with the law, "the kind of scrape any boy might have got mixed into," according to Chauncey, brought him toe to toe with Sheriff Whitehill. Billy fell in with another boarder at Mrs. Brown's, a young stonemason named George Schaefer, nicknamed "Sombrero Jack" on account of his distinctive hat. "Every Saturday night George would get drunk," said Harry Whitehill. "But he thought a lot of Billy and Billy used to follow him around." He was a less than ideal companion for a youngster already giving in to temptation. As Harry put it, "This fellow George liked to steal. He had a mania to steal and he was always stealing."[41]

On Saturday night, September 4, Schaefer broke into the beleaguered Charlie Sun's house and made off with two revolvers and a large bundle of blankets and clothes that

Mary Richards.

belonged to a number of townsfolk, valued from $150 to $200. He hid the booty in the stamp pit at Crawford's Mill in Georgetown, which was not operating at the time. Schaefer could see Billy was poor and needed clothes, so he offered him a share if he ran the risk of bringing the bundle back to town. The youth must have badly needed the clothes to break his promise of good behavior to the sheriff.

Mrs. Brown discovered Billy's role in the heist when she poked her nose into his trunk. On Thursday, September 23, the indignant landlady informed Sheriff Whitehill that the boy, an accessory after the fact, was wearing stolen clothes and hiding stolen property in her house. The sheriff collared him, giving George Schaefer time to skip town with the balance of the stolen goods before Whitehill could learn of his role in the affair.[42]

Billy told his story at a hearing before justice of the peace Isaac Givens. "It's believed that Henry was simply the tool of 'Sombrero Jack,' who done the actual stealing whilst Henry done the hiding," reported the local paper. "Jack has skinned out." Whitehill sympathized, knowing that his own sons were just as bad, if not worse, than Billy. But he agreed with Givens that it was necessary to teach all the boys a lesson by making an example of young Antrim. Charged with larceny, Billy would receive a trial before the grand jury when the circuit court came to town the third week of November. The scheduling meant a long confinement in jail.

Jennie Ramsdell, the sheriff's niece, was visiting when Whitehill came home that night. He told the family what had happened and faced a storm of protest from his kids. "Of course, I put up for Henry," said Jennie. Her uncle told the family that "Henry was getting so wild after his mother's death" that Whitehill "thought that by locking him up for the night it might get Henry to thinking and possibly do him some good." The next morning, the sheriff's wife, Har-

Levi Miller.

riet, who "was very fond of Henry, too," directed her husband to bring the boy home for breakfast.[43]

Billy did not know that Sheriff Whitehill, acquiescing to Harriet and his kids, planned to turn him loose after a few days and offer the hospitality of the Whitehill home. After only two days, he could not sit still. "Billy conceived the idea of escaping," said Anthony Conner, "which I suppose he got from the books he had been reading."

"The Kid complained to me that the jailor was treating him roughly," reported the sheriff,

> and kept him in solitary confinement in his cell without any exercise. So I ordered that he be allowed to remain in the corridor for a limited time each morning . . . for a short half-hour. When we returned and unlocked the heavy oaken doors of the jail, the Kid was nowhere to be seen. I ran outside around the jail and a Mexican standing on a ridge at the rear asked whom was I hunting. I replied, in Spanish, "a prisoner." He came out the chimney, answered the Mexican. I ran back into the jail and looked up into the big, old-fash-

City Meat Market, Silver City.

ioned chimney and sure enough could see where in an effort
to obtain a hold his hands had clawed into the thick layer of
black soot which lined the sides of the flue.[44]

Other prisoners escaped by tunneling through the wall,
filing the bars, or chiseling the window grating, but only Billy
climbed up the chimney. His friends thought his cleverness
was more than the situation called for. They cautioned
against mischaracterizing adolescent rebellion as criminal
behavior. "He was not bad," insisted Louis Abraham, "he was
just scared. If he had only waited until they let him out he
would have been alright, but he was scared and he ran away."

"It did not amount to anything," stated Anthony Conner, "and Mr. Whitehill only wished to scare him . . . to leave
him there alone for awhile so that Billy could realize what
such acts might lead to."

Sheriff Whitehill admired his nerve. "He had a mind
whose ingenuity we knew not of at that time," he said. "He
was only a boy, you must remember, scarcely over fifteen
years of age."[45]

28

Levi Miller's blacksmith shop, c. 1880.

Billy made straight for Clara Truesdell. Convinced that a jail term would ruin the boy, she gave him some of Chauncey's clothes to wear and sent him up to Ed Moulton's sawmill on Bear Mountain. Mrs. Joe Dyer cooked for the lumbermen there. She would look after him until Clara could reason with the sheriff. Clara tried, but she could not prove his innocence. Whitehill and Givens found out where the boy was hiding, "but he managed to get away and come to us," remembered Chauncey, and ". . . mother washed Henry's clothes and dried them by the stove. My brother, Gideon, Henry and I slept on the floor that night. The next morning mother stopped the stage as it passed our door and asked the driver to take Henry to Globe City [actually, Clifton], Arizona. Mother gave Henry all the money she had and a little lunch to eat."[46]

William Henry McCarty, also known as Henry Antrim, was not much older than fourteen when he left Silver City. Those who knew him there agreed that circumstances led him to steal. Billy would not excuse the slightest insult or

29

injustice. When provoked, as in the incident with Levi Miller, his temper forced a confrontation even though his opponents outsized or outnumbered him. As Ash Upson observed, "he could not and would not stay whipped." As he began to get his growth, his bold and mischievous nature sometimes exerted itself and led inevitably to conflict. At such times, his youthfulness and sense of humor usually disarmed the angry party, at least in the beginning.

"There was one peculiar facial characteristic that to an experienced manhunter, would have marked him as a bad man," noted Sheriff Whitehill, "and that was his dancing eyes. They were never at rest, but continually shifted and roved, much like his own rebellious nature." Dick Clark had an innocuous interpretation. "His eyes were those of a person full of fun," he remembered. "He was generous and kind to everyone until someone did him dirt then he would seek revenge."[47]

This was the boy who escaped from the Silver City jail and struck out on his own for the Arizona Territory.

Later, when dime novelists wrote up the adventures of Billy the Kid, they imaginatively filled in the next two years with border raids into old Mexico, a jail break in San Elizaro, and the mass slaughter of Indians, Mexicans, and Chinese, all in the flowery and racist dime-novel tradition. But the most fanciful tale came from the pages of a New York City newspaper. In a ludicrous case of mistaken identity, the *Sun* reported that Billy the Kid had stabbed a drunk to death in a street brawl—in the Fourth Ward ghetto of New York City. Writers ignored the more pragmatic testimony of Billy's contemporaries amidst all this imaginary blood-letting. They agreed on his destination if not his mode of transport. Billy headed west, not east.[48]

"He went to the [Pete] Slaughter ranch in Arizona,"

insisted Louis Abraham, "and that settled it. He never came back again."

"He caught a freight wagon," stated Anthony Conner, "and went to Fort Grant, Arizona."

"My mother put him on the early morning stage for Globe," remembered Chauncey Truesdell.

"Billy's father worked in Arizona," said Harry Whitehill, "and Billy went over there."[49]

Whether by wagon or stage, Billy followed his stepfather to southeastern Arizona. Like many others in Silver City, William Antrim had trailed mineral discoveries to Clifton and the new mining districts of Pinal County. If the boy hoped to find refuge with Antrim, he was disappointed.

When Billy told his stepfather about the trouble he had gotten into, remembered Harry Whitehill, Antrim responded with characteristic indifference: " 'If that's the kind of boy you are, get out.' Now, if Billy's father had taken him in then Billy would have been all right. But he didn't and the kid turned bad. The boy didn't know what to do, so he went up into the old man's room, stole his six-shooter and some clothes, and beat it."[50]

The San Simon Valley of Arizona drew the young adventurer to his main source of income, gambling. The settlements of Safford and Pueblo Viejo offered him the opportunity in saloons and dance halls, as did the recently decommissioned military post of Camp Goodwin. Transients could also find work gathering hay or herding cattle on farms and ranches along the Gila River. The most prominent rancher was Newman H. "Old Man" Clanton, whose extended family formed a community large enough to be called "Clantonville." Along the way, Billy earned the nickname "Kid," an apt description for a high-spirited boy learning to pull his own weight among grown men.

Billy learned that a professionalism with cards compensated for a physique unsuited to manual labor, and that a

Charles Bottom.

familiarity with firearms discouraged troublemakers. He may have hitched a ride on a freight wagon to the Gila Valley. He needed transportation and lacked the means to buy a horse. So, on March 19, 1876, in a forewarning of what was to come, Billy rode off on a horse belonging to Private Charles Smith, who had stopped at Camp Goodwin while traveling on detached service from Camp Grant.[51]

Gambling enticed Billy to the saloons near Camp Grant, situated in the Sulphur Springs Valley below the towering Pinaleño Mountains. He arrived "about April 19," wrote Miles L. Wood, the square-jawed, broad-shouldered, no-nonsense proprietor of Hotel de Luna. His hostelry was an adobe building with four small rooms; he provided meals by day and bunks to sleep in by night. Billy worked as a cook before moving on.[52]

The army allowed only two civilian businesses, the Hotel de Luna and sutlers Norton & Stewart, inside the military reservation. The perimeter ran roughly three miles from the flagpost and followed the road east to Stockton's

Margaret Keays Miller, 1872.

Pass and west into the Aravaipa Valley. A widely scattered assortment of adobe and clapboard civilian enterprises clung to the outskirts, dependent on the army payroll and the annual roundup.

A half-mile down the road from Hotel de Luna, at the crossroads leading south to Tucson or Camp Bowie, stood Milton McDowell's store, George Atkins's cantina, and a blacksmith shop run by Francis P. "Windy" Cahill, a discharged infantryman out of Camp Crittenden. He had received his nickname "because he was always blowin' about first one thing and another," said cowboy Gus Gildea. A quarter-mile away, on the east side of Grant Creek, George McKittrick operated a flourishing red-light district that soldiers dubbed "The Hog Ranch." John Bachelder, a construction worker who built much of the post and its nearby settlement, remembered that "gambling and drinking saloons and dance houses were numerous. A man named Lou Elliott had a dance hall. George Atkins ran another." Patrons consisted of travelers, cowboys from the

Hotel de Luna.

neighboring ranches, and soldiers from Camp Grant.[53]

Here, Billy refined his dexterity at the card table and built up a reputation as a gambler. "There were many noted bad men drifting in and out," reported Bachelder. "Billy the Kid was there for a time, he was a young, light, green-looking fellow." He also ran afoul of the blowhard Windy Cahill. "Shortly after the Kid came to Fort Grant, Windy started abusing him," said Gus Gildea, a cowboy who had ridden in with a John Chisum herd and remained to find other work in the valley. "He would throw Billy to the floor, ruffle his hair, slap his face and humiliate him before the men in the saloon. Yes, the Kid was rather slender. . . . The blacksmith was a large man, with a gruff voice and blustering manner." The quick-tempered youth remembered his mistreatment at Cahill's hand.[54]

Billy worked briefly as a cowboy for Henry C. Hooker, an army contractor whose Sierra Bonita Ranch was less than an hour's ride from Camp Grant. Hooker's general manager, a capable young man named William Whelan, hired Billy but had to let him go soon after. "He was a light-weight," said the Hooker family, unable to perform the labor required of the men. In search of work, Billy probably called on the other ranchers in the valley—Patterson & Diehl, Thomas Hunter, Caleb Martin, George H. Stevens, and "Old Man" Clanton.[55]

Perhaps he found work at one of the roving cow camps belonging to John Chisum, the self-styled "Cattle King of the Pecos" from Lincoln County, New Mexico. Chisum had begun driving cattle into the region in 1873 after the newly formed San Carlos and Chiricahua reservations created a market for beef in Arizona. His herds fattened on ranges near Camp Bowie, at Croton Springs near present-day Willcox, on the San Pedro River near Old St. David, and on the Empire Ranch south of Tucson. He spent the autumn of 1876 situating a large herd on the Eureka Springs Stock Ranch, a new spread north of Hooker's. If Billy did not meet Chisum, he probably sought work at Eureka Springs and made the acquaintance of George Teague, Chisum's foreman.[56]

By November, through a combination of circumstance and habit, Billy finally settled into an occupation that suited his physical abilities and appealed to his sense of adventure: horse stealing. "He got to running with a gang of rustlers," wrote Miles Wood. "This place was the headquarters of the gang." Billy's mentor was John R. Mackie, a twenty-eight-year-old trumpet player whose discharge from the Sixth Cavalry had resulted from a shooting scrape in McDowell's store. "Billy and his chum Mackie would steal the saddles and saddle blankets from the horses," explained Wood. "Occasionally, they would take the horses and hide them out until they got a chance to dispose of them."[57]

Mackie probably arranged with the proprietors of the Hog Ranch to steal horses from their preoccupied customers. He could not keep the scheme a secret for long. Two officers thought they could outwit him. They tied up their horses with long picket ropes and took the ends of the ropes inside the Hog Ranch with them. Mackie also went inside to keep his former superiors occupied. "When they came out they only had a piece of rope in their hands," reported Wood, "and Kid had gone with their horses."[58]

As a result, Major Charles Compton issued a general order declaring the Hog Ranch off-limits to soldiers. It did not take. On November 17, First Sergeant Louis C. Hartman of Company G, Sixth Cavalry, tied his horse "near the store of one M. McDowell." Not necessarily at the store, but at the Hog Ranch, which was *near* the store, on the other side of Grant Creek. When he came out, the mount was gone. Five days later, Major Compton issued another general order sending Hartman, Private Charles Smith, who had lost his mount to Billy in March, and three other privates to pursue the horsethieves.[59]

The military posse tracked the horse through the Aravaipa Valley and into the mountains of Pinal County, where several mining districts centered around booming Globe City on Pinal Creek. Only a few months before, Globe City had been a handful of miners' tents and improvised shelters. Then mineral discoveries drained the male populations of nearby Florence and Silver City, so that by December forty buildings stood and others were going up. The soldiers continued north to the Stonewall Jackson Mine, newly discovered by Charles McMillen, which lay just across the border and inside the San Carlos Reservation. Some twenty miners defied the Apaches and the Indian Agency by pitching their tents in McMillen's Camp. Among them were two men from Silver City, Patrick Shanley—and William Antrim.

On November 25, Hartman and Smith overtook Billy on the trail to the camp. They may not have known who stole the horse until they caught him riding it. Why they did not arrest him is unclear. They unceremoniously

Miles L. Wood.

reclaimed the animal and left the boy to walk back through the hostile country.

Billy probably remained in the district throughout the autumn of 1876 and the early part of 1877. The boy had his choice of twelve saloons in which to play poker and deal monte. He probably tended bar in Isaac's Saloon under the alias of Austin Antrim, a Texas gambler. He might have been the "Texas youth" who drew a bead one night on John Brannaman during an indoor shooting competition. One bullet missed its mark and struck Phineas Clanton in the mouth, punching out two front teeth as it cut a downward swath into his neck. As one newspaper commented, "such is life in new mining camps."[60]

Whenever the cards failed to fall Billy's way, Mackie led him to a source of capital. Late on the night of February 10, 1877, they stole three horses from Cottonwood Springs, a water station on the wagon road near the headquarters of the Norton & Stewart Cattle Company. The horses belonged to Company F stationed at Camp Thomas.

The theft prompted more decisive action from the U.S. Army. On February 16, the quartermaster from Camp Thomas and officers from Camp Grant berated Miles Wood, recently elected justice of the peace for the civilian community adjoining Camp Grant, for not taking action against the horsethieves. Justice Wood held occasional court at his Hotel de Luna. "I hope you are not afraid to go get him," one of the men told him. Stung by the admonishment, Wood told the soldiers to sign a formal complaint so that he could issue arrest warrants. Sergeant Hartman stepped forward and swore out a complaint charging "Henry Antrim alias Kid" with stealing his horse.[61]

Wood sent hand-drawn wanted posters to constables in various districts. He received word from Pinal County that Billy's stepfather was prospecting in McMillen's Camp; the soldiers may have encountered Antrim there the previous November. Wood then sent arrest warrants to law officers in Globe City. They apprehended Billy, but he managed to slip away. The following day, constables caught him again and started the journey back to Camp Grant. They got as far as the Norton & Stewart Cattle Company in Cedar Springs before Billy escaped once more.[62]

At the same time, William Antrim put distance between himself and his wayward stepson, returning to Silver City.[63] From then on, Billy would say contemptuously, "Antrim is my stepfather's name." As if to deny kinship, he resumed the use of his first name, reduced his middle name to an initial, and replaced Antrim with his brother's middle name. William Henry McCarty, temporarily Henry Antrim, was now William H. Bonney.[64]

Billy's narrow escape from the soldiers evidently made him consider the error of his ways. In a gesture that speaks well for him, he resolved his troubles with the army by returning five horses to the acting assistant quartermaster at Camp Thomas, and "the matter was dropped," according to Miles Wood. The justice himself had not dropped it, however, when Billy and Mackie, having squared themselves with the Sixth Cavalry, returned to the saloons near Camp Grant.[65]

George Rothrock, the pioneer photographer who was then touring Arizona military posts, observed the pair's roughhousing near Camp Grant. "I met the noted Billy the Kid and witnessed his having trouble with a friend of his, mounting his horse, a race horse that belonged to his friend, riding off shooting his pistol at him, and the friend firing his Winchester at him."[66]

Thus alerted, Wood placed warrants in the hands of his elderly constable and dispatched him "to arrest the boys. He came back and said he could not find them. I sent him down three times, but he always said he could not find them. I knew he did not want to find them."

A few days later, on the morning of March 25, Wood glanced out the window and saw Billy and Mackie approaching Hotel de Luna. He took it as a direct challenge to his authority when they sat down and ordered breakfast. "I told the waiter I would wait on them myself. I had the breakfast for the two placed on a large waiter [tray] and I carried it in to them," Wood reported. "I shoved the platter on the table in front of them and pulled a sixgun from under it and told them to put up their hands and then to go straight out the door." With the help of the hotel's cook, Caleb Martin, Wood marched them at gunpoint two and a half miles up the road to the post. The sergeant of the guard agreed to lock them up.[67]

Wood sat down to write a letter to Major Compton before convening a coroner's inquest into the recent death of James Wall Lockhart, a Chisum cowboy. A few days before, Lockhart, after sobering up from a drunken carouse with members of the Sixth Cavalry, had accidentally grazed a soldier on the head with a bullet from his Winchester. He endured a severe beating; the soldiers hoisted him onto his horse, and he tried to escape. But a sergeant carefully shot the cowhand out of the saddle, and Lockhart had died three days later. Just before the inquest, Wood asked Compton to confine Billy and Mackie "in the Post Guard-house at Camp Grant until such time as a judicial investigation can be given their cases." His missive completed, the justice of the peace headed to the post hospital.

By noon, Wood had taken forty pages of testimony when a commotion across the parade ground interrupted the proceedings. Billy had asked for permission to use the privy outside. As soon as he and his escort reached the rear of the building, he threw a handful of salt into the guard's eyes and ran toward the creek. Eyes burning, the guard yelled for help and several soldiers came running. Acting with the restraint they had lacked when James Lockhart attempted to escape, the soldiers caught Billy and sent for Justice Wood. It was the last straw. Under Wood's orders— and over Billy's protestations—blacksmith Windy Cahill riveted shackles onto Billy's ankles. Wood put the boy back in the guardhouse.

When the justice returned to the inquest, the soldiers "admitted that whiskey was to blame" for Lockhart's death. Their realization worried the jury. They could not decide if a soldier could commit a homicide while under the influence. Before long, this same perplexed jury would decide Billy's future.[68]

Billy was barely fazed by this new state of affairs. The guardhouse was built of overlapping boards standing upright in a foundation of stone and mud mortar. It had a dirt floor and a wood-shingle roof. The walls were twelve feet tall. Running along the top was a narrow ventilation ridge that the sagging roof had widened.

Globe City, c. 1878.

That evening, while officers and civilians danced to the regimental band in the major's quarters, Mackie boosted his young friend up the wall. Billy squeezed himself through the opening and dropped to the ground outside. He followed the creekbed out of the post, past the Hotel de Luna, and down to Atkins's cantina. There, bartender Tom Varley pried open his shackles while the sergeant of the guard knocked on Major Compton's door. He informed the major and Miles Wood that Billy had escaped again, shackles and all. "He was a small fellow not weighing over ninety pounds," Wood remarked, "and it was almost an impossibility to keep him imprisoned or hand-cuffed."[69]

While Billy was on the loose, trouble was brewing around John Chisum in the Rio Pecos country of New Mexico. It would soon reach Arizona and change the course of Billy's life. Chisum's efforts to save his cattle from wholesale theft had put him "in armed rebellion against other cattle owners and the law." Two of his foremen had been killed in gunfights, in addition to Lockhart, and a third had fled to Texas to escape lynching. In the summer and fall of 1877, Chisum's cowboys drove large herds off the Pecos to secure ranges in southeastern Arizona. They also brought word of an entrenched gun battle on the Pecos with an organized band of rustlers, a battle that Chisum lost.[70]

Billy, looking for work, showed up at the hay camp, near Camp Thomas, of army contractor H. F. "Sorghum" Smith as rumors were spreading that Chisum was hiring gunmen. Smith told an acquaintance about Billy:

> He said he was seventeen, though he didn't look to be fourteen. I gave him a job helping around camp. He hadn't worked very long until he wanted his money. I asked him if he was going to quit. He said, "No, I want to buy some things." I asked him how much he wanted and tried to get him to take $10 for I thought that was enough for him to spend, but he hesitated and asked $40. I gave it to him. He went down to the post trader and bought himself a whole outfit: six shooter, belt, scabbard, and cartridges.[71]

On August 17, a Friday night, Billy wore his new get-up to George Atkins's cantina. Gus Gildea saw him come "to town, dressed like a 'country jake,' with 'store pants' on and shoes instead of boots. He wore a six gun stuffed in his trousers." Gildea watched as the "easy going, likable youth, still in his teens" got into an argument with Windy Cahill, his tormentor. The blacksmith was about to bully the boy over the line from larceny to murder.[72]

Cahill called Billy a pimp, making a confused reference to Mackie's arrangement with the Hog Ranch. Enraged, Billy called the blacksmith a son of a bitch. The fight erupted as Miles Wood happened on the scene. They "got to wrestling to see who could throw the other down," the justice reported. "Cahill was larger and stouter than the Kid and threw him down three times which made the Kid mad." Gildea also watched as Windy "threw the youth to the floor.

42

Pinned his arms down with his knees and started slapping his face. 'You are hurting me. Let me up!' cried the Kid. 'I want to hurt you. That's why I got you down,' was the reply. People in the saloon watched the two on the floor."[73]

Then, observed Gildea, "Billy's right arm was free from the elbow down. He started working his hand around and finally managed to grasp his .45. . . . The blacksmith evidently felt the pistol against his side, for he straightened slightly. Then there was a deafening roar. Windy slumped to the side as the Kid squirmed free." As Wood saw it, Billy "pulled his sixgun and stuck it in the stomach and fired and killed Cahill."[74]

Keeping his presence of mind, Billy ran outside, mounted the best horse within reach, and rode off before anyone could stop him. Cashaw, known as the fastest pony in the valley, carried Billy at a gallop all the way to Clifton before giving out. Billy acquired another mount and sent the prize horse back to its owner, John Murphey. Leaving the scene was wise, considering his past relationship with the law and with Cahill's army friends.

Back at Camp Grant, the blacksmith lay dying from an internal hemorrhage. Wood took down his last words:

> I, Frank P. Cahill, being convinced that I am about to die, do make the following as my final statement . . . yesterday, August 17th, 1877, I had some trouble with Henry Antrem [sic], otherwise known as Kid, during which he shot me. I had called him a pimp, and he called me a son of a bitch; we then took hold of each other. I did not hit him, I think; saw him go for his pistol and tried to get hold of it, but could not, and he shot me in the belly. [75]

Cahill died after giving the statement.

Wood convened an inquest in the Hotel de Luna. With the exception of one T. McCleary, all the jurors had served on the Lockhart inquest just a few months before: brick-

maker James L. "Dobie" Hunt, storekeeper Milton McDowell, sutler Bennett Norton of the Norton & Stewart Cattle
Company, former soldier Delos H. Smith, and Chisum's
Eureka Springs foreman, George Teague. This time Wood
did not record their reasoning, just their verdict: "The
shooting was criminal and unjustifiable, and Henry Antrim
alias Kid, is guilty thereof."[76]

However, some people thought Cahill got what was
coming to him, and saw Billy's act as self-preservation rather
than premeditated murder. If Gus Gildea had been on the
jury, the verdict might have gone the other way. "He had no
choice," Gildea argued. "He had to use his 'equalizer'."[77]

On August 23, Pima County Sheriff William Osborn read
about the shooting in the Tucson *Arizona Citizen*. Probably
to determine the jurisdiction, he telegraphed an inquiry to
Camp Grant. "Cahill was not killed on the reservation,"
Major Compton replied. "His murderer, Antrim alias Kid,
was allowed to escape and I believe is still at large."[78]

"At large" meant on the run back to New Mexico. Even
before Compton and Osborn exchanged communications,
Billy had reached Knight's Station at the southwestern base
of the Burro Mountains. His Silver City friends Richard and
Sara Conner Knight now ran the stage stop, for Richard had
the mail contract. Billy's pal Anthony Conner worked there,
riding a fast horse to deliver the Arizona mail to Ralston and
other settlements in Grant County. "He told the folks what
he had done," remembered Anthony. "He remained there
about two weeks, but fearing that officers from Arizona
might show up any time he left."[79]

Billy read Cahill's deathbed statement and the jury's verdict when the Arizona newspapers arrived. Unlike his
occasional theft of a horse or a saddle, Billy could not undo
Cahill's death, and he must have been aware of the gravity
of the verdict. Because he lacked the means to raise bond,

44

he probably would have had to stay in prison pending a grand jury investigation in criminal court. Then, the "criminal and unjustifiable" verdict virtually assured a conviction of first-degree murder. The sheriff of Pima County, Arizona, had extradited men from New Mexico for lesser offenses, and if an officer was trailing him, he would make his first stop at Knight's Station. Apaches, however, were more of a risk at the moment than pursuing lawmen. Sheriff Whitehill and an outraged citizenry had formed posses to search the mountains for depredating Apaches from the San Carlos Reservation. No one bothered with a boy outlaw.[80]

Wary of Indians, Billy left Knight's station, avoided town, and sought refuge at Ed Moulton's sawmill. The old friend who had helped him once now gave him a cool reception. "He came . . . on a half-starved horse and asked to stay awhile," said Jim Blair. "Billie told Ed the trouble he had gotten into. Ed advised him not to stay too long around his place if he was running from the law. . . . When the boy had fed his horse until he gained some strength he told Ed that he was thinking about drifting over to Lincoln Co. and joining the war."[81]

To a rootless boy with a thirst for excitement, the prospect of fighting in a civilian conflict must have been irresistible. The same Silver City and La Mesilla newspapers that reported the shooting of Windy Cahill alerted people to the ongoing activities of "the Banditti of New Mexico," the title bestowed on a band of rustlers raising havoc across the southern half of the territory. Now they threatened John Chisum's cattle drives into Arizona. Employed by Chisum's competitors and led by his former trail drovers, Jessie Evans and Frank Baker, the Banditti were reportedly cutting out cattle on the fringes of moving herds, claiming to have resold them in advance at $10 a head. Another armed clash seemed unavoidable, and people were taking sides. Ed

Moulton asked Billy "which side he was going to join, but the boy didn't know."[82]

He made up his mind at Apache Tejoe, a busy overnight stop that served travelers on the road that joined Silver City to settlements on the Rio Grande. A man named Hog Davis had built the prosperous farm on the ruins of old Fort McLane. From here, Billy maintained a safe distance from the law while keeping a watchful eye on traffic. The Banditti passed by, too, following a horse-stealing raid in Lincoln County on September 18. Billy met Jessie Evans and his men: Frank Baker, George Davis, Tom Hill, George Spawn, a man called Mose, and two Indians, Ponciano and Manuel Segobia, among others. His new compadres made him "a hardened character," said Louis Abraham. "Billie had no reason, only fear, for he hung around Apache Tejo [sic] quite a while, and Sheriff Whitehill could have gotten him if he had wanted him punished." The outlaws seemed to enjoy immunity from the law, and their rough fellowship was a near-guarantee that Billy would not get caught.[83]

In late September Billy went looking for his brother, Joe. He found him with Chauncey Truesdell on Charley Nicolai's ranch, on the Mimbres River northeast of Georgetown, where they had fled to escape the threat of smallpox at the Truesdells'. Early one morning, the younger boys were just in the act of taking about "half a tomato can of milk" from a reluctant cow, said Chauncey, "when three men came riding into the corral." Two of them were Indians with red bands tied around their hats. "That is the way the Indians had of showing they were peaceful," Chauncey commented. He went on:

> I can well remember how carefully Joe sat the milk can down on the floor and came up with an old Henry rifle and was about to take a shot at the leader, who called to Joe to "hold on Joe, don't you know your own brother?" It was

Henry and he stayed and visited Joe that night and after sending best regards to mother, they went away by way of Bear Canyon. That was the last I ever saw of Henry Antrim.[84]

William Henry McCarty was already forgotten. Henry Antrim now introduced himself as William H. Bonney. Sheriff Whitehill thought he had "changed his name in order to keep the stigma of disgrace from his family." Old friends who saw him in the fall of 1877 observed a new maturity. The boy who had fled New Mexico for the offense of wearing stolen clothes now returned a seasoned survivor of the frontier, versed in lawlessness and hardened to violence, but still a boy in personality and appearance. Barely over sixteen years old, he was already trading on the survival skills he had learned. Making his own way had brought out a self-reliance and a willingness to dare anything. Eager for adventure, the newly christened William H. Bonney rode with the Banditti into Lincoln County.[85]

Notes

1. Most books about Billy the Kid are reconstructions of legends and myths. If Billy the Kid is a myth, then the subject of this book is William Henry McCarty, the actual person.

For reliable research into Billy's origins, read the following: Philip J. Rasch and Robert N. Mullin, "New Light on the Legend of Billy the Kid," *New Mexico Folklore Record*, vol. 7 (1952-1953), pp. 1-5; Rasch and Mullin, "Dim Trails: The Pursuit of the McCarty Family," ibid., vol. 8 (1953-1954), pp. 6-11; Rasch, "More on the McCartys," *The Brand Book Quarterly* (London: English Corral of the Westerners, April 1957), pp. 3-9; Rasch, "Clues to the Puzzle of Billy the Kid," ibid. (December 1957-January 1958), n.p.; Rasch, "And One Word More," *Brand Book*, vol. 8 (Chicago: Chicago Corral of the Westerners, August 1961), pp. 41-42; Rasch, "Old Problem—New Answers," *New Mexico Historical Review*, vol. 40 (January 1965), pp. 65-67; and Waldo E. Koop, *Billy the Kid: The Trail of a Kansas Legend* (Wichita: Kansas City Posse of the Westerners, 1965).

For opinions where the evidence doesn't support the conclusions, see [William J.] Kit Carson, "Who Was Billy the Kid's Mother?" *Real West*, vol. 7 (September 1964), pp. 14-17, 49-50; William J. Carson, "What Was Billy the Kid's Real Name?" ibid., vol. 12 (May 1969), pp. 46-48; Jack DeMattos, "The Search for Billy the Kid's Roots," ibid., vol. 21 (November 1978), pp. 12-19, 39; DeMattos, "The Search for Billy the Kid's Roots—Is Over!" ibid., vol. 23 (January 1980), pp. 26-28, 59-60; Donald R. Cline, *Alias Billy the Kid: The Man Behind the Legend* (Santa Fe: Sunstone Press, 1986); and Frederick Nolan, *The Lincoln County War: A Documentary History* (Norman: University of Oklahoma Press, 1992), pp. 3-9, 527.

2. William Antrim and Catherine McCarty's wedding is recorded twice: in Marriage Record 1863-1899, pp. 35a-36, Santa Fe County Records, New Mexico State Records Center and Archives (NMSRCA), Santa Fe, New Mexico; and in Book of Marriages, p. 164, Santa Fe County Courthouse. Both documents provide persuasive evidence that Catherine was a widow (they both name her as "Mrs. Catherine McCarty"); that her sons were known by her first married name, McCarty; that their names were Henry and Joseph; and that the family had been residing in Santa Fe. Another witness, Harvey Edmonds, frequently witnessed marriages in the Presbyterian church.

Other sources with data on the family's arrival in New Mexico are

Daily New Mexican (Santa Fe), July 10, 1881; *Daily Journal* (Albuquerque), July 20, 1881, p. 4, col. 3; and *Independent* (Silver City), July 21, 1908.

3. The person born William Henry McCarty was known by a combination of names during his brief life. For continuity and simplicity, this work refers to him as "Billy," but quotations may refer to him by his other appellations.

4. Dick Clark interview by Mrs. W. C. (Frances E.) Totty, November 15, 1937, WPA Files, History Library (HL), Museum of New Mexico (MNM), Santa Fe. Ed Moulton Biographical File, Silver City Museum (SCM), New Mexico. Susan Berry, director of the Silver City Museum, is working on a biography of Ed Moulton, which promises to give important new information.

Arthur Stockbridge remembered hearing from William Antrim, an Old Man Mimms, and Ed Moulton that Billy and his stepfather were working for a blacksmith, who one day insulted Catherine when Billy had brought lunch to Antrim. Billy jumped on the blacksmith's back and stabbed him to death. As will become apparent, this story confuses several different incidents. Arthur Stockbridge interview by Robert N. Mullin, March 29, 1961, in Billy the Kid Binder, Robert N. Mullin Papers (RNMP), J. Evetts Haley History Center (HHC), Midland, Texas. F. Stanley recorded more "Kid stories of later vintage" in *The Georgetown, New Mexico Story* (Privately printed: May 1963), p. 9.

5. Susan Berry and Sharman Apt Russell, *Built to Last: An Architectural History of Silver City, New Mexico* (Santa Fe: New Mexico Historic Preservation Division, 1986). Conrad Keeler Naegle, "The History of Silver City, New Mexico 1870-1886" (M.A. thesis, University of New Mexico, 1943).

For books that touch incidentally on Billy's time in Silver City, see H. B. Ailman, *Pioneering in Territorial Silver City: H. B. Ailman's Recollections of Silver City and the Southwest, 1871-1892*, ed. and annot. by Helen J. Lundwall (Albuquerque: University of New Mexico Press, 1983), and O. W. Williams, *Pioneer Surveyor, Frontier Lawyer: The Personal Narrative of O. W. Williams, 1877-1902*, ed. by S. D. Myres (El Paso: Texas Western College Press, 1966).

6. Emigrants from Chicago, Denver, and Utah and their effects on the town are reported in *Mining Life* (Silver City), June 7, 1873, p. 3, col. 1; July 12, 1873, p. 1, col. 5; July 19, 1873, p. 3, col. 1; and in *Tribune* (Silver City), October 18, 1873, p. 6, col. 1. Rendell Rhoades letter to Lena Shaw, January 23, 1872, John Swisshelm Biographical File, SCM.

The publication of several spurious photographs of the Antrim cabin have created confusion about its location and appearance. William Antrim filed on lots 4 and 6, block 16 of the R. M. Kidder plat on June 10, 1874. See Deed Book 2, pp. 514-17, County Clerk's Office, Grant County Courthouse (GCC), Silver City, New Mexico. Authenticated photographs show a small, oblong cabin at this intersection. See Photograph

#198 (c. 1878) and Photograph #554 (c. 1875), John Harlan Collection, SCM. It occupied lot 2, or the first lot on the block. *The Independent*, July 21, 1908, places the home on this site. Therefore, there is no mystery as to the location and configuration of the Antrims' cabin during the time they lived in it.

Sanborn insurance maps made years after the Antrims vacated the cabin conflict with misidentified photographs. The maps also indicate that the structure underwent a succession of alterations before it was moved or obliterated by floods. Neither maps nor photographs show the cabin during the time the Antrims occupied it. For two misidentified cabins, see Negative #99054, MNM; and photograph section between pages 14 and 15 of Robert N. Mullin, *The Boyhood of Billy the Kid*, Southwestern Studies Monograph No. 17 (El Paso: Texas Western Press, 1967). Sanborn insurance maps, 1883, 1886, 1893, 1898, Science and Engineering Library, University of New Mexico (UNM), Albuquerque.

To further complicate the matter, after Billy's death souvenir-hunting newspapers gave conflicting and inaccurate data on the cabin. See *Southwest Sentinel* (Silver City), March 21, 1883, p. 3, col. 3; March 24, 1883, p. 3, col. 2; and March 28, 1883, p. 3, col. 1. *Enterprise* (Silver City), June 23, 1889, p. 3, col. 1, and December 7, 1894, p. 3, col. 2. For an incredible contrivance of all of the above, see Cline, "The Mystery of Billy the Kid's Home," *Quarterly of the National Association and Center for Outlaw and Lawman History [NOLA Quarterly]*, vol. 13 (Fall 1989), pp. 15-19.

Main Street was prone to flooding. In 1895 a series of floods scooped out the dirt road and swept away all the buildings. The site of the Antrim cabin became an arroyo, and the arroyo became a canal now known as "The Big Ditch." A park is located along its banks. See Berry and Russell, *Built to Last*, pp. 39-40, 57-59.

7. I reconstructed the neighborhood and the environment from Deed Book 1 and Deed Book 2, GCC; A. Z. Huggins, 1873 town diagram, Geography and Map Division, National Archives (NA), Washington, D.C., copy in SCM; John R. Fraser survey of Silver City, December 17, 1879, Deed Book 4, GCC; photographs of the town c. 1872 - c. 1878, SCM; random issues of *Mining Life* and *Tribune*; *Grant County Herald* (Silver City), June 6, 1875, p. 3, col. 1.

The Star Hotel had been the Nevada Hotel; it was soon to be the Exchange Hotel, later the Timmer House. Bennett's store was later the Southern Hotel, operated by Louis Abraham. The Keystone Hotel was later called the Tremont House.

8. Chauncey O. Truesdell interview by Robert N. Mullin, January 9, 1952, Billy the Kid Binder, RNMP. It is difficult to separate Truesdell's statements from the journalists' embellishments in *Daily Press* (Silver City), May 23, 1951, p. 12, col. 1; Roscoe G. Willson, "Billy the Kid's Youth is Topic for Argument," *Arizona Republic*, December 30, 1951, section 3, p. 3, col. 1; and "Outlaw's Globe Career Clouded with Rumor," ibid., January 6, 1952, section 3, p. 3, col. 1. Louis Abraham interview by

Frances E. Totty, November 23, 1937, WPA Files, HL. For a corroborative account in Abraham's own hand, see Louis Abraham letter to Maurice G. Fulton, April 22, 1932, Research Notes: Billy the Kid—Antrim Folder, RNMP.

9. Abraham interview; Clark interview. There has been considerable debate as to whether Catherine kept a boardinghouse. When asked if she had a hotel, oldtimers said no; the same oldtimers said that she kept a boardinghouse. The confusion derives in part from a misunderstanding of the term "boardinghouse." It does not mean a hotel, it means affording beds and meals for pay. In view of her circumstances, it would be surprising if Catherine did not take in a boarder whenever she could. I am convinced that she did. There is also a possibility that after her death, Antrim rented the cabin. He didn't sell his adjoining lots to Joseph Buhlman until April 24, 1876. Deed Book 2, p. 515.

10. Abraham interview. Dan Rose, "Early Days of the Great Southwest," *Independent*, June 12, 1917, p. 5.

11. Abraham interview. Wayne Whitehill interview by Louis Blachly, April 3, 1952, Pioneer's Foundation Recordings (PFR), Zimmerman Library, UNM. Charles E. Stevens in Marie Stevens Miliken, "Bonanza Bound: Isaac James Stevens and His Experiences as a Pioneer," manuscript, courtesy of Harvey H. Whitehill III, copy in author's files. Wayne Whitehill and Stevens tell and confirm some of the boys' names; the rest can be deduced.

Charley and his brother Al later moved to Clifton and became prominent pioneers of that mining town. The Greenlee County Historical Society in Clifton held their collections of family papers and photographs for fifty years. Their reminiscences were said to contain much about Silver City and Billy. No one made use of the material before the 1983 flood that destroyed the museum building and all its collections. For a capsule biography of Stevens, see *History of Arizona*, 4 volumes (Phoenix: Record Publishing Co., 1930), vol. 3, pp. 378-79.

Dan Rose, who later moved to Globe and Ajo, wrote two books on Arizona history and a newspaper serial on the early days of Silver City. He is also said to have written a manuscript about Billy the Kid, but there is no trace of it. Out of this group of wild kids, Billy is the only one who did not grow up to be a substantial citizen in the community.

12. Truesdell interview; "Former Resident" letter to *Enterprise*, August 29, 1902, identifies himself only as Jack, a former soldier of Company E, Fifteenth Infantry, stationed at Fort Bayard.

13. This composite description is assembled from Harvey H. Whitehill interview in *Enterprise*, January 3, 1902, p. 1, col. 1; "Former Resident" to ibid., August 29, 1902; Abraham, Emma Whitehill Kilburn, and Harry Whitehill interviews, by Helen Wheaton, September 3, 4, 1928, "Semi-

Centennial Celebration," typescript, Historical Files (HF), SCM; Wayne Whitehill interview; Chauncey O. Truesdell Reminiscence, September 29, 1950, BF, SCM; Truesdell interview; Anthony B. Conner letter to *Independent*, March 22, 1932, p. 1, col. 6; Frank B. Coe, "A Friend Comes to the Defense of the Notorious Billy the Kid," *El Paso Times* (Texas), September 16, 1923; and an interview with Coe in Miguel Otero, *The Real Billy the Kid: With New Light on the Lincoln County War* (New York: Rufus Rockwell Wilson, 1936), pp. 145-46.

14. Scott's eloquent editorials on "book learning" are in *Mining Life*, May 31, 1873, p. 1, cols. 4 and 5; July 15, 1873, p. 4, cols. 1 and 2; July 26, 1873, p. 4, cols. 2 and 3; August 9, 1873, p. 3, col. 2; and January 6, 1874, p. 3, col. 1. For the meaning of "Village Arabs," see Eric Partridge, *The Penguin Dictionary of Historical Slang* (New York: Penguin Books, 1972), p. 29.

15. *Tribune*, September 13, 1873, p. 5, col. 1; September 27, 1873, p. 3, col. 2; October 11, 1873, p. 6, col. 1; November 22, 1873, p. 6, col. 1. *Mining Life*, November 15, 1873, p. 3, col. 2; April 11, 1874, p. 3, col. 2; July 24, 1874, p. 3, cols. 1 and 2.

16. *Mining Life*, June 21, 1873, p. 3, col. 2; August 9, 1873, p. 3, col. 1. This William Wilson should not be confused with the William Wilson who rode with Billy following the Lincoln County War.
Ash Upson, Pat Garrett's ghostwriter, built an enduring legend on this incident. To fabricate Billy killing his first man, Upson substituted Billy the Kid for Wilson and Ed Moulton for Dyer. Pat F. Garrett, *The Authentic Life of Billy, the Kid, The Noted Desperado of the Southwest* (Santa Fe: New Mexican Printing and Publishing Co., 1882), pp. 10-11. For another real crime that writers later exaggerated and blamed on Billy, see note 35.
For David Abraham, see *Tribune*, September 20, 1873, p. 6, col. 1; November 8, 1873, p. 5, col. 1. For the jail, see ibid., August 22, 1873, p. 5, col. 1; September 6, 1873, p. 5, col. 2; and *Mining Life*, August 9, 1873, p. 3, col. 2; August 30, 1873, p. 3, col. 2; February 14, 1874, p. 3, col. 2.

17. Unfortunately, this school census does not list names. *Mining Life*, November 19, 1873, p. 4, col. 1; January 3, 1874, p. 3, col. 1; January 10, 1874, p. 3, col. 2; February 21, 1874, p. 3, col. 3; April 4, 1874, p. 3, cols. 2 and 3. *Grant County Herald*, January 1, 1876, p. 3, cols. 2 and 3. Because Joseph Antrim is also listed, it is likely that while he appeared older, he was actually younger than Billy. The school was open only to those under sixteen years of age. Danny and Tommy Rose are also listed.

18. Louis Abraham and Harry Whitehill interviews. Miliken, "Bonanza Bound." "I went to school with Billy the Kid," concurred Wayne, the youngest Whitehill. Actually, Wayne was too young to be a pupil, but wherever big brother and sister Harry and Emma went, Wayne

was sure to follow. Wayne Whitehill interview. In 1929 Charles E. Stevens gave his account of his childhood to his friend Albie Anderson, another Clifton pioneer, who then conveyed it to Almer Blazer. Albie Anderson, "Billy the Kid Story," attached to letter to Almer Blazer, October 31, 1931, Blazer Family Papers, Rio Grande Historical Collections (RGHC), New Mexico State University (NMSU), Las Cruces.

19. Harry Whitehill and Kilburn interviews. Their reminiscence matches an obscure contemporary newspaper item, *Mining Life*, February 6, 1874, p. 3, col. 1.

20. *Mining Life*, February 7, p. 3, col. 1; March 28, p. 4, cols. 3 and 4; June 20, p. 3, col. 2; July 11, p. 3, cols. 3 and 4, all 1874. Three troupes— youngsters, adults, and blacks—regularly held minstrel shows in Silver City. The absurd story of Billy the Kid performing female roles in the Silver City Opera House originated in 1967. It was invented to market a collection of photographs, which appeared in Mullin, *Boyhood of Billy the Kid*. Further, the building that housed the Silver City Opera House wasn't built until 1886, ten years after Billy left town and five years after he died. It did not become the Opera House until 1888. See 1883, 1886, 1888, 1893, and 1898 Sanborn maps.

21. Harry Whitehill interview.

22. *Mining Life* reports on Shanley's delivery and the jail on December 27, 1873, p. 3, col. 1; January 24, 1874, p. 3, col. 2; February 14, 1874, p. 3, col. 2; and on the theft, March 14, 1874, p. 3, col. 2.

23. In *Authentic Life of Billy, the Kid*, p. 4, Garrett notes, "I am in daily intercourse with one friend who was a boarder in the house of 'the Kid's' mother, at Silver City." The friend, of course, was Garrett's ghostwriter, Ash Upson. Historians have disregarded Upson's claim to being a boarder in the Antrim cabin because of his inauthentic account of Billy's life. However, Upson's presence in Silver City and his prospecting trip through Grant County from March through May of 1874, with his partner Leslie T. Anderson, are documented in the newspaper and in letters to Upson's niece, Florence Muzzy. *Mining Life*, March 21, 1874, p. 3, col. 2. Leslie T. Anderson letter to Dear Lady [Florence Muzzy], May 26, 1874; Ash Upson letter to Florence Muzzy, undated because the first page is missing, but written after May 26, 1874; both in Maurice G. Fulton Papers (MGFP), Folder 5, Box 11, Special Collections (SC), University of Arizona Library (UAL), Tucson. Further, Upson's eyewitness description of Catherine is in Garrett, *Authentic Life of Billy, the Kid*, pp. 8-9. See also Jim Blair (Ed Moulton's son-in-law) interview by Totty, December 10, 1937, WPA Files, HL.

24. Miliken, "Bonanza Bound." *Tribune*, September 6, 1873, p. 2, col. 1. Despite all evidence to the contrary, Donald Cline paints a sordid pic-

ture of Catherine throughout his book *Alias Billy the Kid*, casting every conceivable aspersion on mother and sons. The base nature of the book probably accounts for its popularity. His accusations are unsupported by his evidence.

25. Truesdell interview.

26. *Mining Life*, May 2, p. 3, col. 1; May 9, p. 3, col. 1; June 6, p. 3, col. 1; August 8, p. 3, cols. 1 and 3; August 15, p. 3, col. 1, all 1874.

27. The Mexican circus is in ibid., May 30, 1874, p. 3, col. 1. Billy's attempted robbery is in *New Southwest and Grant County Herald* (Silver City), February 25, 1882; Wayne Whitehill interview; Anderson to Blazer. Catherine's words are in James H. East to Edward M. Dealey, *Dallas Morning News*, c. 1922. Billy repeated Catherine's remark to East, a deputy of Pat Garrett's, when Garrett and East apprehended Billy near Fort Sumner in December 1880.

The American troupe, Blackenstose's Circus, set up their big top in the intersection of Broadway and Bullard, a stone's throw from the Antrim cabin, but free of the rain water that muddied up Main Street. The three-day visit excited the county and went without incident: "The sight of a veritable circus tent set the juvenile hearts to palpitating and with open-mouthed wonder witnessed the preparations for the evening's entertainment," noted the paper. "But the prevailing question, 'Ma, can we go to the show?' seemed to have been answered in the affirmative, for the tent was crowded . . . and the juveniles were well pleased." *Mining Life*, August 8, p. 3, cols. 1 and 3; August 15, p. 3, col. 1, 1874.

28. Truesdell Reminiscence; Truesdell interview; Abraham interview. Catherine's obituary is in *Mining Life*, September 19, 1874, p. 3, col. 3.

There has been confusion over the headstone and cemetery location, with two cemeteries and three different markers. The cemetery originally occupied a two-block area bounded on the north by Twelfth Street, on the east by Santa Rita Street, on the south by Tenth Street, and on the west by West Street, placing it squarely within town limits. By 1880 it was in the northern end of town. See Deed Book 4, March 13, 1882. When the state legislature passed a law prohibiting cemeteries within town limits, John A. Miller, post sutler at Fort Bayard, proposed moving the bodies to the second hill northeast of town in exchange for a deed to the present property. See *Grant County Herald*, February 6, 1876, and *New Southwest and Grant County Herald*, September 10, 1881; January 7, 14, 1882. When Miller moved the bodies in January of 1882, he replaced some of the wooden crosses with wooden headboards. When transferring the inscription from the cross to the headboard, he misspelled Catherine's name as "Kathrine" and misdated her death as September 8. The headboard gave her date of birth as 1829, which might also be an error. The mistakes may have originated with William Antrim. His disinterest in his family was still evident even in the 1910s, when he answered questions about them on his pension affidavits, RG 94, NA. In the 1920s, Maurice G. Fulton photographed the headboard before weather obliterated the carved writing.

In 1947, Sidney H. Curtis and S. Ernest Pollack of the Curtis-Bright Funeral Home donated the fine granite stone that corrected the date of her death (but not her name) and now marks her grave, on Cypress Lane in Memory Lane Cemetery. In 1951, Raymond McCune acquired the 1882 headboard from L. C. Raines, caretaker of Memory Lane, and donated it to New Mexico State Monuments. It has been on exhibit in the Tunstall Store Museum in Lincoln ever since. See Sidney H. Curtis and S. Ernest Pollack interviews by Robert Mullin, July 9, 1952, in Research Notes, RNMP; and Mullin, "A Grave Question," *Password*, vol. 17 (Winter 1972), pp. 173-74.

29. Agnes Meador Snider interview by Louis Blachly, March 29, 1952, PFR. Snider said that at Antrim's death, his cousin Lon Irish inherited his trunk, which contained a large sum of hoarded money. Irish and Antrim boarded in her Mogollon home for many years.

Contrary to the dime-novel image, William Antrim, fondly known as Uncle Billy in his senior years, was not an abusive parent.

30. Conner to *Independent*. For corroborative accounts written by Conner, see his letters to Maurice G. Fulton, April 29, June 26, 1932, Folder 2, Box 1, MGFP.

31. Truesdell Reminiscence; Truesdell interview. Olive Whitehill Bell is quoted in Bernie Paca, " 'The Kid' Was Just Another Brat to Silver City's Sheriff Whitehill—Before Billy Became Famous," *The Southwesterner*, vol. 2 (August 1962), p. 5. Philip J. Rasch, "The Quest for Joseph Antrim," *NOLA Quarterly*, vol. 6 (July 1981), pp. 13-17.

32. *Mining Life*, April 11, p. 3, col. 3; September 12, p. 3, col. 1, and September 26, p. 3, col. 2, all 1874.

33. For Mary Richards's account see two articles by William C. McGaw, "Out of the West: Mutiny, Fire at Sea, Yellow Fever Combined to Provide Teacher for Billy the Kid," *Herald-Post* (El Paso), December 10, 1960, and "Out of the West: Billy the Kid's Teacher Saw Him as Sensitive, Effeminate and Fearful Youth," ibid., December 17, 1960. Her daughter, Patience Glennon, reluctantly gave this interview in her Silver City home in December of 1960. She also read and approved the text prior to publication, so we may take it as a reliable account of what her mother told her. For an elaboration, see two more articles by McGaw, "Billy the Kid Gets Teacher by Accident," *The Southwesterner*, vol. 1 (May 1962), p. 3, and "Billy the Kid's Teacher Saw Him as a Fearful 'Sissy'," ibid., vol. 1 (June 1962), pp. 15-16.

34. *Mining Life*, October 31, p. 3, col. 1; November 5, p. 3, col. 1;

November 14, p. 3, cols. 1 and 2; all 1874. To add to Johnson's worries, on the night of Thursday, November 19, someone stole a blanket from her line. "The person who stole the blanket from my line is known," she announced, "and will be prosecuted unless the blanket is returned, in which case nothing will be done about it." On Friday, December 4, she shot at an unidentified intruder who, it turned out, returned the blanket. Ibid., November 21, p. 3, col. 3; December 5, p. 3, cols. 1 and 3, both 1874.

35. In fact, a member of the Village Arabs did kill a Chinese man in Silver City. In a emotional outburst on the tape recording, Wayne Whitehill recounted that the boys were in the habit of throwing rocks at the Chinese, and that Manuel Taylor, who was a little older than the other boys, killed a Chinese immigrant with a rock when the boys were competing to see who was the best thrower. However, Whitehill's chronology is confused, placing the incident during the time Billy ran with the Village Arabs (1873-1875). The incident actually occured on August 17, 1879, a Sunday, and Billy was not involved, having left Silver City four years earlier. According to the *Grant County Herald*, August 23, 1879, p. 3, col. 1, "This is the first Chinaman that has died in our town." Because it falls within the 1870s, it must be the killing Wayne Whitehill remembered. Charley Stevens confirmed the incident in Miliken, "Bonanza Bound." Wayne Whitehill interview; Louis Abraham interview. Conner to *Independent*.

Much later, journalists who caught wind of the local gossip simply attributed the deed to Billy the Kid. In a fictitious interview entitled "The Dead Desperado: Adventures of Billy the Kid," Billy sells a stolen keg of butter to a Chinese man, who betrays him to the town sheriff. After his arrest, Billy escapes up the chimney and gets revenge by cutting the Chinese man's throat. The "interview" ran as a serial on the front page of *Las Vegas Daily Optic*, September 12-21, 1882. It is probably the origin of the oft-repeated story that Billy killed a Chinese laundryman.

36. *Mining Life*, December 19, 1874, p. 3, col. 2; January 6 or 16, 1875, p. 3, col. 1; February 6, 1875, p. 3, col. 1.

37. In 1880 in Silver City there were an R. H. Brown, barkeeper, and his wife, Sarah A. Brown, whose occupation was "boarding." In August of 1873 people named Brown and O'Brien were building a brick cottage on Main Street, north of Seventh. Sarah was probably the Mrs. Brown that Chauncey remembered. *Mining Life*, August 30, 1873. 1880 Census, Grant County, New Mexico, SC. *Independent*, July 21, 1908. Truesdell Reminiscence. Truesdell interview.

Unnamed Silver City resident interview by Betty Reich, April 2, 1937, WPA Files, HL. The typescript of this interview begins naming Billy then switches to a "youth," substantiating the widely held belief that the WPA interviewers and transcribers were often inept. The story about Billy—"a youth"—working for Bottom is probably true. It is consistent with his liking for good horses, and with his other employment. Further, it is in character for him to take foolish risks and, if we can believe other eyewitnesses, be helpful. It is easy to scoff at Billy doing good deeds, but they appear in all the eyewitness testimony.

In the 1950s, researcher Rasch heard a lurid story from an oldtimer named H. A. Hoover, in which Billy beheads a kitten with a newly purchased Barlow jackknife given to him by Antrim. Although such work is consistent with a butcher's chores, butchers did not serve catmeat. The ghoulish behavior is out of character. The story has no antecedent or corroboration, but it has become a favorite of writers with an anti-Billy the Kid bias who make no effort to evaluate it. Philip J. Rasch, "A Man Named Antrim," *The Westerners Brand Book*, vol. 6 (Los Angeles Corral of the Westerners, 1956), p. 51. Philip J. Rasch to Jerry Weddle, August 22, 1992, author's files.

38. *Independent*, July 21, 1908. Charley Stevens told of Billy's gambling skills in Anderson, "Billy the Kid Story."

According to Ash Upson, Billy tried to strike a loafer with a rock for insulting his mother as she passed by on the street, then tried to shoot him, but Ed Moulton intervened. There may be some truth to it, but Upson is so adept at mixing fact and fabrication that it cannot be taken at face value. Garrett, *Authentic Life of Billy, the Kid*, p. 10.

Persistent oral tradition in Silver City tells of Miller provoking Billy. Lucile Gray interview by Jerry Weddle, March 1988, author's files. Gray heard the story from Margaret Keays Miller. It should be noted here that Lawrence E. Gay, the dealer, misidentified a photograph of Margaret Keays Miller as Catherine Antrim in Mullin, *Boyhood of Billy the Kid*. See Jerry Weddle interview by Denise Zendel, "Information Sought on Billy the Kid's Mother," *Roswell Daily Record*, February 21, 1990, p. 8. Abraham interview. Conner to *Independent*. Clark interview; Blair interview.

39. Harvey H. Whitehill interview.

40. Abraham interview; Blair interview; Clark interview; Conner to *Independent*; Silver City resident interview.

41. Truesdell interview; Harry Whitehill interview. Schaefer was later a justice of the peace in Georgetown. Truesdell and Whitehill both named Schaefer as the thief, but the papers named only "Sombrero Jack." This may have been the editor's sly method of pointing a finger at the culprit without the risk of naming names.

42. *Grant County Herald*, September 5, 1875, p. 3, col. 1. Truesdell interview; Harry Whitehill interview. Sheriff Whitehill remembered Billy stealing $70 from a Chinese man in Georgetown. Perhaps this was a different theft, or the dollar value of the clothes. Harvey H. Whitehill interview.

43. There appears to be no legal paper on the crime. The newspaper

reported that Billy was in jail waiting for the grand jury, but no charges against him appear in the docket books for Grant County. Further, although there are voluminous justice of the peace records, it does not appear that Isaac Givens kept records this early. Perhaps Givens and Whitehill dropped the matter before they formally filed charges. District Court Docket Books, Grant County, NMSRCA. Jennie (Ramsdell) Van Wagenen in Ross Santee, *Lost Pony Tracks* (New York: Charles Scribner's Sons, 1953), pp. 249-51. Jane (known as Jennie) Ramsdell was the daughter of Susan Stevens Ramsdell, Charley Stevens's eldest sister. She married a Globe pioneer, Garrett Van Wagenen. In his book, Santee misspelled her name as "Van Wagonen."

44. Conner to *Independent*; Harvey H. Whitehill interview. Billy's escape is in *Grant County Herald*, September 26, 1875, p. 3, col. 3. There are interesting variations on the jail break. Harry Whitehill said that Schaefer was arrested with Billy, and they escaped together. He added that Schaefer had been a worker on the jail and that he "took out some big rocks over the fireplace and boosted the Kid up." Jennie Van Wagenen heard that her uncle had arrested two Mexican boys for petty thieving with Billy and that her uncle did not think Billy was in with them on the theft. An unidentified resident of Silver City also said that someone escaped with Billy. Harry Whitehill to Wheaton; Santee, *Lost Pony Tracks*, pp. 249-51; Silver City resident interview.

45. Abraham interview. Conner to *Independent*; Harvey H. Whitehill interview. Reports of previous escapes are in *Mining Life*, June 20, p. 3, col. 3; July 11, p. 3, col. 3; September 19, p. 3, col. 1; all 1874.

46. Chauncey concluded, "The name of the driver was Ben Sincere [St. Cyr]." Truesdell Reminiscence; Truesdell interview. Willson, "Billy the Kid's Youth is Topic for Argument."

47. Garrett, *Authentic Life of Billy, the Kid*, p. 9. Harvey H. Whitehill interview; Clark interview.

48. Garrett, *Authentic Life of Billy, the Kid*, pp. 13-17. *New York Times*, September 10, p. 12, col. 2; September 11, p. 8, col. 3; September 29, p. 5, col. 5; all 1876. *New York World*, September 10, 1876, p. 1, col. 5. *New York Sun*, September 10, 1876, p. 1, col. 6.
A Michael McCarthy stabbed to death one Thomas Moore in New York City on September 9, 1876. He eluded the police, and it was believed that his father sent him on a boat back to Ireland. Five years later, when his friends and neighbors read the obituaries of Billy the Kid, they imagined that McCarthy had escaped to New Mexico and become the notorious outlaw. Their story, "Claiming Billy the Kid," appeared in *New York Sun*, July 22, 1881, p. 1, col. 7. *New York World*, July 26, 1881, and *Daily Optic* (Las Vegas, New Mexico), July 30, 1881, effectively repudiated this obvious case of mistaken identity, but it caught on in the wake of

sensational stories following Billy's death. Newspapers reprinted it end-lessly, including *Arizona Weekly Star* (Tucson), July 28, 1881, p. 1, col. 2.

Cline, *Alias Billy the Kid*, pp. 15-21, 37-41, tries to make a case for McCarthy being McCarty by fabricating a birth record and manipulating other evidence. It requires so much side-stepping and omitting that the book reads more like a burlesque than a historical reconstruction. Michael McCarthy was not William Henry McCarty/Antrim. See also William Thorndale, "Billy the Kid and the New York Murder," *NOLA Quarterly*, vol. 16 (September 1992), p. 32.

49. Abraham interview. Pete Slaughter had the PS Ranch near Springerville, then in Yavapai County. He is not to be confused with John Slaughter, rancher and lawman in Cochise County. Conner to *Independent*; Truesdell Reminiscence; Truesdell interview; Harry Whitehill interview.

50. Harry Whitehill interview. Oral tradition in the Antrim family holds that Antrim's first job as a miner was "in the Carlisle Mine near Duncan, Arizona." Rasch, "A Man Named Antrim," p. 49. The trouble is that Duncan did not exist in the early 1870s, and the Carlisle Mines were in New Mexico, not Arizona. However, at this time many Silver City pioneers were extending their operations to Clifton, then to the Longfellow Copper Mines, and, several years later, to Duncan. Antrim and the Abraham, Stevens, and Whitehill families were all involved in early Clifton. Many residents of Silver City had businesses in Clifton, and many of them moved there. Further, it was easy to get there, for Silver City serviced Clifton with a scheduled stage line and a continuous flow of freight wagons. For a description of Clifton as a new camp populated largely by miners from Silver City, see *Tribune*, September 20, 1873, p. 2, col. 2.

51. Mullin, *Boyhood of Billy the Kid*, pp. 14-15. The theft is in Record of Events column, entry for Company G, Sixth Cavalry, Post Returns, Fort Grant, Arizona, March 1876, Returns from U.S. Military Posts 1800-1916, M-617, Roll 415, NA. Billy's theft of Smith's horse is inferred by Smith's part in the posse in November. See note 61.

The Whitehill family holds that Billy ambushed a soldier to get the horse, but the action is out of character and lacks hard evidence. See Harvey H. Whitehill interview; Harry Whitehill interview; and the "Billy the Kid Story" attached to Anderson to Blazer letter.

52. Miles L. Wood Reminiscences, 1911 and 1923, photocopy in author's files. Miles L. Wood interview, *Tucson Citizen* (Tucson), December 23, 1901, p. 8, col. 3. An advertisement naming Wood as the proprietor of Hotel de Luna appears in Richard J. Hinton, *Hand-book to Arizona: Its Resources, History, Towns, Mines, Ruins and Scenery* (San Francisco: Payot, Upham & Co., 1878), p. lvii.

An inquiry form from the Office of the Arizona Historian prompted Wood to write his reminiscences in July 1911. He filled it out and sent it in, but there was more to tell. He began to reminisce about Billy on a scrap of paper torn from his ledger. He continued writing on a full page in a thick lead pencil. In a second draft, he switched to ink and ruled paper and made an effort to improve phrasing and punctuation. He wrote at length, but only three pages dealt with Billy. In 1923 his young grandson, Mark DuBois, needed a paper for school, so Wood wrote a third account, "Memories of Old Bonita." Finally, in the late 1920s, he collaborated with his daughter, Leslie Wood Quinn, on an unfinished memoir that she called "Life Notes of M. L. Wood," photocopy in author's files. Each manuscript offers details not found in the other, and each is worded slightly differently, but they are all consistent and convey essentially the same facts. No doubt more of Wood's writings are gathering dust in the closets of various descendants.

53. Wood Reminiscences; Quinn, "Life Notes of M. L. Wood." Some of Leslie Wood Quinn's story also appears in William R. Ridgway, "Number Two for Billy," *The Sheriff Magazine*, vol. 10 (December 1956), pp. 67-69; and Ridgway, "Billy the Kid Killed First at Bonita," *Journal of Graham County History*, vol. 5 (1969), pp. 5-7.

This reconstruction of the Camp Grant precinct is assembled from a section map showing original landowners, DuBois family files; Arizona Census, 1874, 1876, 1878, in Arizona Department of Library, Archives and Public Records (ADLAPR), Phoenix; Poll Lists of Electors, Tally Sheets, precinct of Camp Grant, 1874, 1876, in Miscellaneous Pima County Territorial Records (MPCTR), volume 53; and Great Registers for Pima County, 1874, 1876, both in SC, UAL.

Wood Reminiscences. John R. Bachelder interview by Mrs. George F. (Edith) Kitt, 1925, Arizona Historical Society (AHS), Tucson. Irene F. Kennedy interview by author, February 17, 1987. Walking tours of the area, February, March, April, August 1987, with Dorothy DuBois and Henrietta DuBois, who inherited the land from Miles Wood. Known as Bonita since 1887, the community no longer resembles its frontier origins with the exception of the McDowell building, later Knowler & Johnson's, then the DuBois Mercantile Company, now the Bonita Store. In 1965 the Graham County Historical Society photographed the ruins of the Hotel de Luna. In 1983 floods obliterated the foundation.

Cline, *Alias Billy the Kid*, p. 152, asserts that Wood could not have occupied land on the military reservation because he was a civilian. Actually, his presence there became a controversial issue on June 25, 1876, when the acting assistant adjutant general inspected the reservation. See Major James Biddle, Inspection Report and appendices, RG 159, NA.

The quote about Cahill is from cowboy Gus Gildea. Journalist J. Fred Denton filtered Gildea's eyewitness account through an article titled "Billy the Kid's Friend Tells for First Time of Thrilling Incidents," *Tucson Daily Citizen*, March 28, 1931, p. 20, col. 1.

54. Bachelder interview. Denton, "Billy the Kid's Friend." Part of the interview was reprinted in *Tombstone Epitaph*, April 2, 1931, p. 1. Gildea

was John Chisum's foreman on the drive in November 1876, and he remained in the region to work for Hooker. See Rasch, "Gus Gildea—An Arizone [sic] Pioneer," *Brand Book*, vol. 23 (London: English Corral of the Westerners, Summer 1985), pp. 1-7.

For more on Windy Cahill, see Allan Radbourne and Rasch, "The Story of 'Windy' Cahill," *Real West*, vol. 28 (August 1985), pp. 22-27. Francis P. "Windy" Cahill should not be confused with John F. Cahill, also a blacksmith, who served with John G. Bourke and later went into business in Pinal County.

55. Bachelder interview; Wood Reminiscences; Kennedy interview. Dorothy and Henrietta DuBois interviews by author, February, March, April, August 1987, author's files. On July 1, 1876, census-taker Charles A. Shibell listed "William Kidd" with the names of the other Hooker cowboys in the Precinct of Camp Grant, sound evidence of Billy working for Hooker. See Arizona Census, 1876. Charles Whelan telephone conversation with author, March 19, 1987, author's files. Charles Whelan is the grandson of William Whelan. For ninety-seven years, from 1872 to 1969, the Whelans managed the Hooker ranch. The quote is from Jacqueline A. Hughes interview by author, April 19, 1987, author's files. She is the last surviving member of the Hooker family. Ledgers at the ranch listing employees and accounts are said to contain Billy's name, but the volumes for 1875, 1876, and 1877 have not been made available to this researcher.

An oft-repeated story by B. E. "Cyclone" Denton has Billy working on the Gila Ranch, originally a stagecoach stop near Casa Grande that was abandoned after 1868 when Indian depredations forced the Butterfield stage line to cease operations. The ranch no longer existed by the time Billy came to Arizona. However, if Denton was referring to a ranch on the Gila River, then the PS Ranch below Springerville may qualify. See an interview with Denton in Ramon F. Adams, "Billy the Kid's Lost Years," *Texas Monthly*, vol. 4 (September 1929), pp. 205-211.

Rasch unearthed a local legend that finds Billy in St. Johns, Arizona, and involves a hold-up and Billy stealing a valuable racing mare. See Rasch, "A Billy the Kid Incident?," *NOLA Quarterly*, vol. 4 (Summer 1978), pp. 6-7.

56. John Chisum's extensive ranching operations in southeastern Arizona have never been adequately researched, but a wealth of evidence proves he was in the same place at the same time as Billy. A selective list: *Daily New Mexican* (Santa Fe), January 20, 1877, p. 1, col. 3, mentions Chisum's stay in Arizona from October 1876 to January 1877; Gus Gildea, "Experiences of a Ranger and Scout," in J. Marvin Hunter, *The Trail Drivers of Texas*, 2 volumes (Bandera: Old Timer Trail Drivers' Association, 1923), vol. 2, pp. 421-32, gives Gildea's account of a November 1876 Chisum drive into Arizona; and Ming Family Papers, MS 547, AHS. Daniel H. Ming was one of the earliest settlers in the Aravaipa Valley and its first postman, had charge of the ranch when George H. Stevens owned it, and

knew its history firsthand. He wrote that Chisum started the Eureka Springs Stock Ranch as a relay camp. Ross Calvin, *River of the Sun: Stories of the Storied Gila* (Albuquerque: University of New Mexico Press, 1946), p. 136, mentions a Chisum drive to the Aravaipa Valley in November of 1876.

George Teague's association with the ranch and Chisum is in *Arizona Weekly Star*, August 30, 1877, p. 3, col. 1; *Silver Belt* (Globe), January 24, 1879, p. 1, col. 1; and Lily Klasner, *My Girlhood Among Outlaws*, ed. by Eve Ball (Tucson: University of Arizona Press, 1972), pp. 290, 294, which also refers to Chisum drives into Arizona. Chisum's ledger of accounts with military posts in Arizona is in Lily Klasner Papers, Folder 18, Box 9, Brigham Young University, Provo, Utah, and is excerpted in Klasner, *My Girlhood*, p. 290. William A. Keleher, *The Fabulous Frontier: Twelve New Mexico Items* (Albuquerque: University of New Mexico Press, 1960), p. 60, mentions Chisum's contract with Ewing and Curtiss of Tucson. Pay vouchers for Chisum foremen and subcontractors are in Letters Received by the Office of Indian Affairs 1824-1881, Arizona Superintendency 1863-1880, M-234, Rolls 14-19, NA.

57. Wood Reminiscences; Quinn, "Life Notes of M. L. Wood." Mackie was born on July 21, 1849, in Glasgow, Scotland. In 1862 he enrolled as a musician in Company G, 13th Maryland Infantry Volunteers. After serving three months, he was held as a prisoner of war, then was honorably discharged at Baltimore in May of 1865. He dropped out of sight until 1870, when he re-enlisted in Company G, Sixth Cavalry, in Pennsylvania. Sent to Arizona, he wounded a T. R. Knox in a fight at McDowell's store. He was confined to the post guardhouse until a civil trial exonerated him of attempted murder on grounds of self-defense. Discharged in 1876, he took to petty larceny. Records do not indicate what action the military took after he helped Billy to escape. He re-emerged in 1879, when he re-enlisted at Fort Walla Walla, Washington Territory. In 1896 he moved to Milwaukee, Wisconsin, where he died in 1920. *Arizona Citizen*, September 25, 1875, p. 2, col. 4; October 29, 1875, p. 3, col. 2. Pension affidavits, RG 94, NA.

58. Wood Reminiscences.

59. General Orders for Camp Grant from October 1876 through September 1879 are not in NA, so I must rely on Quinn, "Life Notes of M. L. Wood." Richard F. Cox, Military Reference Branch, Military Archives Division, NA, letter to Jerry Weddle, April 6, 1988. The theft and pursuit are in Absences from Post and Record of Events columns, entry for Company G, Regimental Returns, Sixth Cavalry, November 1876, Returns from Regular Army Cavalry Regiments 1833-1916, M-744, Roll 63, NA. The circumstances of the theft are in Louis Hartman complaint to Miles L. Wood, February 16, 1877, photocopy in author's files.

60. *Grant County Herald*, December 2, 1876, p. 1, col. 4; January 20,

1877, p. 2, col. 4; February 17, 1877, p. 3, col. 2; March 31, 1877, p. 3, col. 3. Robert Bigando, *Globe, Arizona: The Life and Times of a Western Mining Town, 1864-1917* (Globe: American Globe Publishing Company, 1989), pp. 20-30. In the 1930s, historian Clara T. Woody recorded Patrick Shanley's story. The oral tradition corroborates the evidence in note 59, of which Shanley and Woody were unaware. See Clara T. Woody and Milton L. Schwartz, *Globe, Arizona* (Tucson: Arizona Historical Society, 1977), p. 31.

Billy returned to Arizona briefly in 1879 to sell stolen cattle to Shanley, who in turn delivered them on his beef contract to the quartermaster at San Carlos Reservation. See Thomas Cruse, *Apache Days and After* (Caldwell, Idaho: Caxton Printers, 1941), pp. 39-41.

In one of the most popular later-day stories, Billy the Kid shoots and kills his first victim, a Chinese laundryman, in Globe City. No such incident appeared in the papers or in any surviving court records. The Chinese were not in the region this early. The census enumerated the district twice but listed no Chinese residents. See entries for Globe City and Globe Mining District, Arizona Census 1876, Pima and Pinal Counties, and Pinal County public records, all in ADLAPR.

61. Wood Reminiscences; Hartman complaint. The warrants that Wood mentioned have not been found. The theft is in Record of Events column, entry for Company F, Sixth Cavalry, Post Returns, Fort Thomas, Arizona, February 1877, M-617, Roll 1265; entry for Company F, Record of Events column, Regimental Returns, Sixth Cavalry, February 1877.

62. The Wood family has an oral tradition about the hand-drawn wanted posters. Kathy Quinn letter to Jerry Weddle, February 1992, author's files. Wood Reminiscences.

63. "Mr. Antrim has returned from Pinal," tersely announced the *Grant County Herald*, February 24, 1877, p. 3, col. 2.

64. The quote is from a letter from William H. Bonney to General Lew Wallace, n.d. [March 13, 1879], Lincoln County Heritage Trust, Lincoln, New Mexico. Willson, "Billy the Kid's Youth is Topic for Argument."

65. Five horses were reported returned. Entry for Company F, Sixth Cavalry, Record of Events column, Post Returns, Sixth Cavalry, Fort Thomas, February 1877. Quinn, "Life Notes of M. L. Wood," identifies Billy as the one who returned the horses. The thefts occurred from November 1876 through February 1877. There is no evidence to suggest that Billy stole horses and saddles outside of this time frame.

66. George H. Rothrock, "The Life History of George H. Rothrock," August 17, 1924, p. 12, typescript, Rothrock Biographical File, Arizona Historical Foundation, Arizona State University Library, Tempe. For a similar account of Billy's riding stunts, see Klasner, *My Girlhood Among Outlaws*, p. 174.

67. Wood Reminiscences. In "Life Notes of M. L. Wood," Leslie Wood Quinn drapes a napkin over the tray.

68. Wood Reminiscences. The original letter is in Box 4, Letters and Telegrams Received 1873-1905, Fort Grant, Arizona, RG 93, NA.
Lockhart's death is in *Grant County Herald*, March 31, 1877, p. 3, col. 3; and *Arizona Citizen*, March 31, 1877, p. 3, col. 2. Miles L. Wood sent his coroner's report to *Arizona Citizen*, April 7, 1877, p. 2, col. 2. The civil trial is reported in ibid., April 14, p. 3, col. 2; and April 21, p. 3, col. 3, both 1877.

69. Wood Reminiscences. Major Charles E. Compton's January 1877 description of the post buildings is in Irwin McDowell, *Outline Descriptions of Military Posts in the Military Division of the Pacific* (Presidio of San Francisco Headquarters, California, 1879), pp. 7-10. Many secondhand accounts mistakenly place Billy's escape from the guardhouse after Cahill is shot, and follow it with a shootout. Eyewitnesses Wood, Bachelder, and Gildea give the correct chronology but do not mention any shootouts. Wood's quote is from his interview in *Tucson Citizen*, December 23, 1901.

70. *Weekly Arizona Miner* (Prescott), July 13, 1877, p. 1, col. 5; *Grant County Herald*, October 30, 1877, p. 4, col. 1.

71. *Tucson Daily Citizen*, February 4, 1932, p. 7, col. 1. There are many contradictions in this round-table discussion with a group of oldtimers, one of whom, Robert M. Boller, recounted Smith's memories of Billy. The description of Billy's age, personality, and appearance is consistent with those of other people who knew the boy then. Smith, a government contractor, was best known for his sorghum, thus his nickname, also spelled "Sawgum." This article misstated his initials as "J. W.," and so they have appeared in many articles thereafter.

72. Denton, "Billy the Kid's Friend."

73. Wood Reminiscences. Denton, "Billy the Kid's Friend."

74. Ibid. Curiously, though both Gildea and Wood witnessed Cahill's killing, neither mentioned the other in his account.

75. Wood sent Cahill's deathbed statement to *Arizona Weekly Star*, which ran it on August 23, 1877, p. 3, col. 1. Bachelder interview. For more on John Murphey and his horse Cashaw, see Denton, "Billy the Kid's Friend," and two largely fictitious stories by Bernice Cosulich, "Bonita, the One-Time Roaring Camp," *Arizona Daily Star*, April 17, 1932, and "Fort Grant Gives Frontier Sanctuary," ibid., April 24, 1932.

76. Wood sent his coroner's inquest to the *Arizona Citizen*, which

ran it on August 25, 1877, p. 3, col. 2. *Grant County Herald*, September 1, 1877, p. 1, col. 4, and *Mesilla Valley Independent* (Mesilla), September 1, 1877, p. 3, col. 3, reprinted it.

A variety of hand-me-down versions have garbled the essential facts of the Cahill shooting through the years. Dime novelists merged the killing of the blacksmith with the killing of a Chinese man, both in Silver City or Globe City. After 1933, the arrest and escape from the guardhouse occur after Cahill's death. This error originated in a letter from Wood's friend Anton Mazzanovich, who simply confused the order of events. The published letter prompted a response from the son of quartermaster Gilbert Smith, who compounded the confusion by imposing an unrelated incident involving the theft of a freight wagon by teamsters. Actually, it was a supply wagon stolen by deserters. See Fort Grant post returns and correspondence files, RG 93, NA. Thus appeared the endlessly repeated misstatement that Billy was a teamster who stole a wagon. See Anton Mazzanovich, "Tony Tells About the Kid," *Tombstone Epitaph*, March 9, 1933, p. 3, col. 3; and C. C. Smith letter to editor Walter H. Cole, "Editors Mail-bag," ibid., March 30, 1933, p. 4, col. 2.

In two popular pieces by Donald Cline, Billy the Kid kills the wrong Cahill at the wrong Camp Grant. See Cline, "Did Billy-the-Kid Kill Frank Cahill?" *NOLA Quarterly*, vol. 10 (Winter 1986), pp. 15-18, and Cline, *Alias Billy the Kid*, pp. 46-53.

77. Quoted in Mullin, *Boyhood of Billy the Kid*, p. 16.

78. *Arizona Citizen*, August 23, 1877. Compton's telegram to Osborn, telegram copy book, entry 594, p. 111, Fort Grant, Arizona, Part 5, Letters Sent January 1877-May 1878, Vol. 35, Stock 9WZ 10:18C, RG 393, NA.

79. Conner to *Independent*. Conner to Fulton, Folder 2, Box 1, MCFP. Conner told the newspaper that Billy stayed "for about two weeks," but he told Fulton that he stayed "for three or four days." The timing is crucial in reconstructing Billy's activities and whereabouts. In both versions, he stayed at Knight's Station. For more on Conner, see Anthony B. Conner and Sister Mary J. Conner Swan, "Reminiscences of Southwestern New Mexico," unpublished manuscript, BF, SCM.

80. Billy probably knew George Arlington and Joseph L. Crump, who were apprehended in Silver City for selling cattle stolen from Hooker's ranch. Crump escaped, but Sheriff Whitehill delivered Arlington to Tucson authorities under an escort. *Arizona Citizen*, April 8, 1876, p. 3, col. 1. There was also the case of José Cordova, who, on February 14, 1876, stole a horse, bridle, blanket, and violin from Camp Grant and hastened to Silver City. Sheriff Whitehill received a letter from the owner and jailed Cordova pending "requisition" from Arizona authorities. *Grant County Herald*, February 20, p. 3, col. 2; February 27, p. 3, col. 2, both 1876.

81. Blair interview.

82. *Weekly Arizona Miner*, April 21, 1877, p. 2, col. 4. *Arizona Citizen*, July 21, 1877, p. 2, col. 2. *Grant County Herald*, July 21, 1877; September 1, 1877, p. 1, col. 4; October 6, 1877, p. 3, col. 2; October 13, 1877, p. 1, col. 4, and p. 3, col. 1. *Mesilla Valley Independent*, June 23, 1877; July 14, 1877, p. 2, col. 1; July 21, 1877, p. 2, col. 4, and p. 3, col. 2; August 11, 1877; August 25, 1877, p. 3, col. 2; September 1, 1877, p. 3, col. 2, and p. 3, col. 3; September 22, p. 3, col. 2; October 6, 1877, p. 3, col. 2; October 20, 1877, p. 2, col. 3. Blair interview.

83. Apache Tejoe is described in *Tribune*, September 20, p. 3, col. 2; September 27, p. 3, col. 1; and November 22, p. 3, col. 3, all 1873. Abraham interview.

84. Truesdell Reminiscence; Truesdell interview. Truesdell gives substantially the same account in both sources. His chronology in the interview is confused, placing this incident before Billy went to Arizona instead of before he went to Lincoln County.

85. Harvey H. Whitehill interview. Several sources are reproduced in books and articles. Robert F. Kadlec, *They "Knew" Billy the Kid: Interviews with Old-Time New Mexicans* (Santa Fe: Ancient City Press, 1987), prints the Clark interview, pp. 6-7; Abraham interview, pp. 1-4; Blair interview, pp. 12-13; and Silver City resident interview, pp. 5-6. Miles Wood's interview in *Tucson Citizen*, December 23, 1901, is reproduced in Larry D. Ball, "Billy the Kid—the Cook?" *Mid-South Folklore*, vol. 3 (Spring 1975), pp. 25-26. The 1925 John R. Bachelder interview by Edith Kitt at AHS is also in *Arizona Republican* (Phoenix), April 10, 1940.

For a perceptive analysis of Billy the Kid mythology, see Stephen Tatum, *Inventing Billy the Kid: Visions of the Outlaw in America, 1881-1981* (Albuquerque: University of New Mexico Press, 1982). For a fine factual biography, see Robert M. Utley, *Billy the Kid: A Short and Violent Life* (Lincoln: University of Nebraska Press, 1989).

Bibliography

NEWSPAPERS

Arizona

Arizona Citizen (Tucson)
Arizona Daily Star (Tucson)
Arizona Republic (Phoenix)
Arizona Weekly Star (Tucson)
Hoof and Horns (Prescott)
Tombstone Epitaph
Tucson Citizen
Tucson Daily Citizen
Silver Belt (Globe)
Weekly Arizona Miner (Prescott)

New Mexico

Daily Journal (Albuquerque)
Daily New Mexican (Santa Fe)
Daily Optic (Las Vegas)
Daily Press (Silver City)
Enterprise (Silver City)
Grant County Herald (Silver City)
Independent (Silver City)
Las Vegas Daily Optic
Mesilla Valley Independent (Mesilla)
Mining Life (Silver City)
New Southwest and Grant County Herald (Silver City)

Roswell Daily Record
Southwest Sentinel (Silver City)
Tribune (Silver City)

Texas

Dallas Morning News
El Paso Times
Herald-Post (El Paso)

New York

New York Sun
New York Times
New York World

ARTICLES

Adams, Ramon F. "Billy the Kid's Lost Years." *Texas Monthly* 4 (September 1929): 205-211.

"Arizona Early Days: Some Reminiscences." *Tucson Citizen* (December 23, 1901).

Bachelder, John L. "Trip to State Fraught With Many Hazards." *Arizona Republic* (April 10, 1940).

Ball, Larry D. "Billy the Kid—The Cook?" *Mid-South Folklore* 3 (Spring 1975): 25-26.

Bell, Bob Boze. "Billy the Kid." *Arizona Highways* 67 (August 1991): 4-11.

"Billy the Kid Model Youth in Silver City, Says Boyhood Chum." *Independent* (March 22, 1932).

Blake, Herbert Cody. "Billy the Kid, Garrett and Hickok Walk Again." *Tombstone Epitaph* (March 2, 1933).

"Boller Meets Billy the Kid in Tombstone." *Tucson Daily Citizen* (February 4, 1932).

Brent, William. "The Kid in Arizona." *Arizona Republic: Arizona Days and Ways Magazine* (May 15, 1966): 7-10.

Byus, George A., Sr. "Billy the Kid Sells Cattle." *Arizona Daily Star* (February 9, 1929).

————. "Billy the Kid Was Generous." *Arizona Daily Star* (January 13, 1929).

Carson, William J. "Kit." "What Was Billy the Kid's Real Name?" *Real West* 12 (May 1969): 46-48.

————. "Who Was Billy the Kid's Mother?" *Real West* 7 (September 1964): 14-17, 49-50.

Cline, Donald. "Did Billy-the-Kid Kill Frank Cahill?" *Quarterly of the National Association and Center for Lawman and Outlaw History* 10 (Winter 1986): 15-18.

————. "The Mystery of Billy the Kid's Home." *Quarterly of the National Association and Center for Lawman and Outlaw History* 13 (Fall 1989): 15-19.

Coe, Frank B. "A Friend Comes to the Defense of the Notorious Billy the Kid." *El Paso Times* (September 16, 1923).

Corle, Edwin. "Billy the Kid in Arizona." *Arizona Highways* 30 (February 1954): 2-5, 34-35.

Cosulich, Bernice. "Bonita, the One-Time Roaring Camp." *Arizona Daily Star* (April 17, 1932).

————. "Fort Grant Gives Frontier Sanctuary." *Arizona Daily Star* (April 24, 1932).

Cureton, Gilbert. "Knight's Stage Stop Hosted Billy the Kid." *The Southwesterner* 2 (July 1962): 1-2.

"Dead Desperado: Adventures of Billy the Kid as Narrated by Himself." *Las Vegas Daily Optic* (December 12-21, 1882).

DeMattos, Jack. "The Search for Billy the Kid's Roots." *Real West* 21 (November 1978): 12-19, 39.

————. "The Search for Billy the Kid's Roots—Is Over!" *Real West* 23 (January 1980): 26-28, 59-60.

Denton, J. Fred. "Billy the Kid's Friend Tells for First Time of Thrilling Incidents." *Tucson Daily Citizen* (March 28, 1931).

"Early Friend of Billy the Kid Says 'Bandit' Was a Good Boy." *Daily Press* (May 23, 1951).

"Editors Mail-bag: Concerning the Capture of Billy the Kid." *Tombstone Epitaph* (March 30, 1933).

Egerton, Kearney. "The Country Jake Who Became Billy the Kid." *The Arizona Republic: Arizona* (February 13, 1977): 56-57.

"Fanning the Hammer: How Harry Pumped it Into the Tenderfoot." *Hoof and Horns* (March 31, 1887).

Forrest, Earle R. "The Fabulous Sierra Bonita." *Journal of Arizona
   History* 6 (Autumn 1965): 132-146.

Haystead, Ladd. "Modern Bandit Chasing." *Progressive Arizona* 7
   (November 1928): 8-9, 28.

Hinton, Harwood P. "John Simpson Chisum, 1877-1884." *New
   Mexico Historical Review* 31 (July, October 1956): 177-205,
   310-337; 32 (January 1957): 53-65.

Kildare, Maurice. "Saga of the Gallant Sheriff." *The West* 9
   (August 1968): 26-29, 52-57.

Mazzanovich, Anton. "Tony Tells About the Kid." *Tombstone Epitaph* (March 9, 1933).

McGaw, William C. "Billy the Kid Gets Teacher by Accident." *The
   Southwesterner* 1 (May 1962): 3.

———. "Billy the Kid's Teacher Saw Him as a Fearful 'Sissy'." *The
   Southwesterner* 1 (June 1962): 15-16.

———. "Out of the West: Billy the Kid's Teacher Saw Him as Sensitive, Effeminate and Fearful Youth." *Herald-Post* (December
   17, 1960).

———. "Out of the West: Mutiny, Fire at Sea, Yellow Fever Combined to Provide Teacher for Billy the Kid." *Herald-Post*
   (December 10, 1960).

Mullin, Robert N. "A Grave Question." *Password* 17 (Winter
   1972): 173-174.

Mullin, Robert N., and Charles E. Welch, Jr. "Billy the Kid: The
   Making of a Hero." *Western Folklore* 32 (April 1973): 104-111.

Naegle, Conrad K. "The Rebellion of Grant County, New Mexico
   in 1876." *Arizona and the West* 10 (Autumn 1968): 225-240.

Paca, Bernie. " 'The Kid' Was Just Another Brat to Silver City's
   Sheriff Whitehill—Before Billy Became Famous." *The Southwesterner* 2 (August 1962): 3, 5.

Radbourne, Allan, and Philip J. Rasch. "The Story of 'Windy'
   Cahill." *Real West* 28 (August 1985): 22-27.

Rasch, Philip J. "And One Word More." *Brand Book 8* (Chicago
   Corral of the Westerners, August 1961): 41-42.

———. "A Billy the Kid Incident?" *Quarterly of the National Association and Center for Outlaw and Lawman History* 4 (Summer 1978): 6-7.

———. "The Bonney Brothers." *Frontier Times* 39 (December-January 1965): 43, 60-61.

———. "Clues to the Puzzle of Billy the Kid." *The Brand Book Quarterly* (English Corral of the Westerners, December 1957-January 1958).

———. "Gus Gildea—An Arizone [sic] Pioneer." *The Brand Book* (English Corral of the Westerners) 23 (Summer 1985): 1-7.

———. "A Man Named Antrim." *The Westerners Brand Book 6* (Los Angeles Corral of the Westerners, 1956): 49-54.

———. "More on the McCartys." *The Brand Book Quarterly* (London: English Corral of the Westerners, April 1957): 3-9.

———. "Old Problem—New Answers." *New Mexico Historical Review* 40 (January 1965): 65-67.

———. "The Quest for Joseph Antrim." *Quarterly of the National Association and Center for Outlaw and Lawman History* 6 (July 1981): 13-17.

———. "Sidelights on Billy the Kid." *Quarterly of the National Association and Center for Outlaw and Lawman History* 8 (Autumn 1983): 2-7.

Rasch, Philip J., and Robert N. Mullin, "New Light on the Legend of Billy the Kid." *New Mexico Folklore Record* 7 (1952-1953): 1-5.

———. "Dim Trails: The Pursuit of the McCarty Family." *New Mexico Folklore Record* 8 (1953-1954): 6-11.

Ridgway, William R. "Bad Day at Bonita." *The Arizona Sheriff* 17 (July-August 1963): 33-36.

———. "Billy the Kid Killed First at Bonita." *Journal of Graham County History* 5 (1969): 5-7.

———. "Number Two for Billy." *The Sheriff Magazine* 10 (December 1956): 67-69.

Rose, Dan. "Early Days of the Great Southwest." *Independent* (May 29, June 5, June 12, June 19, June 26, July 3, 1917).

"Sheriff Whitehill Was the First Officer to Arrest Billy the Kid." *Enterprise* (January 3, 1902).

"Silver City Years Ago: Former Resident of the City Tells of Stirring Times in Early '70's." *Enterprise* (August 29, 1902).

Thorndale, William. "Billy the Kid and the New York Murder." *Quarterly of the National Association for Outlaw and Lawman History* 16 (September 1992): 32.

White, Richard. "Outlaw Gangs of the Middle Border: American Social Bandits." *Western Historical Quarterly* 12 (October 1981): 387-408.

Willson, Roscoe G. "Billy the Kid's Youth is Topic for Argument." *Arizona Republic* (December 30, 1951).

———. "More About 'The Kid'." *Arizona Republic: Arizona Days and Ways, the Arizona Republic Magazine* (November 18, 1956): 28-29.

———. "Outlaw's Globe Career Clouded with Rumor." *Arizona Republic* (January 6, 1952).

Zendel, Denise. "Information Sought on Billy the Kid's Mother." *Roswell Daily Record* (February 21, 1991).

BOOKS

Adams, Ramon F. *Burs Under the Saddle: A Second Look at Books and Histories of the West.* Norman: University of Oklahoma Press, 1964.

———. *A Fitting Death for Billy the Kid.* Norman: University of Oklahoma Press, 1960.

———. *More Burs Under the Saddle: Books & Histories of the West.* Norman: University of Oklahoma Press, 1979.

Ailman, H. B. *Pioneering in Territorial Silver City: H. B. Ailman's Recollections of Silver City and the Southwest, 1871-1892.* Edited and annotated by Helen J. Lundwall. Albuquerque: University of New Mexico Press, 1983.

Berry, Susan, and Sharman Apt Russell. *Built to Last: An Architectural History of Silver City, New Mexico.* Santa Fe: New Mexico Historic Preservation Division, 1986.

Bigando, Robert. *Globe, Arizona: The Life and Times of a Western Mining Town, 1864-1917.* Globe: American Globe Publishing Company, 1989.

Bishop, William M. *Colorado Families: A Territorial Heritage.* Denver: Colorado Genealogical Society, 1981.

Burns, Walter Noble. *The Saga of Billy the Kid*. Garden City, New York: Doubleday, Page & Co., 1926.

Calkins, Helen M. *The Public Schools of Silver City, New Mexico: A History of the School from 1874 to 1928*. N.p., 1928.

Calvin, Ross. *River of the Sun: Stories of the Storied Gila*. Albuquerque: University of New Mexico Press, 1946.

Cline, Donald R. *Alias Billy the Kid: The Man Behind the Legend*. Santa Fe: Sunstone Press, 1986.

Cruse, Thomas. *Apache Days and After*. Caldwell, Idaho: The Caxton Printers, Ltd., 1941.

Dykes, Jeff C. *Billy the Kid: The Bibliography of a Legend*. Albuquerque: University of New Mexico Press, 1952.

Garrett, Pat F. *The Authentic Life of Billy, the Kid, the Noted Desperado of the Southwest*. Santa Fe: New Mexican Printing and Publishing Co., 1882.

Haines, Helen. *History of New Mexico from the Spanish Conquest to the Present Time, 1530-1890*. New York: New Mexico Historical Publishing Co., 1891.

Hamilton, Patrick. *The Resources of Arizona*. Prescott: Territorial Legislature, 1881.

Hertzog, Peter. *Little Known Facts About Billy the Kid*. Santa Fe: Press of the Territorian, 1963.

Hinton, Richard J. *Hand-book to Arizona: Its Resources, History, Towns, Mines, Ruins and Scenery*. San Francisco: Payot, Upham & Co., 1878.

Hodge, Hiram C. *Arizona As It Is; or, The Coming Country*. New York: Hurd and Houghton; Boston: H. O. Houghton, 1877.

Hunter, J. Marvin. *The Trail Drivers of Texas*. 2 volumes. Bandera: Old Timer Trail Drivers' Association, 1923.

Jernado, Don [John Woodruff Lewis]. *The True Life of Billy the Kid*. New York City: Frank Tousey, 1881.

Kadlec, Robert F., ed. *They "Knew" Billy the Kid: Interviews with Old-Time New Mexicans*. Santa Fe: Ancient City Press, 1987.

Keleher, William A. *The Fabulous Frontier: Twelve New Mexico Items*. Albuquerque: University of New Mexico Press, 1960.

Klasner, Lily. *My Girlhood Among Outlaws*. Edited by Eve Ball. Tucson: University of Arizona Press, 1972.

Koop, Waldo E. *Billy the Kid: The Trail of a Kansas Legend.* Wichita: Kansas City Posse of the Westerners, 1965.

L'Aloge, Bob. *The Code of the West.* Las Cruces: B & J Publications/Yucca Tree Press, 1992.

McDowell, Irwin. *Outline Descriptions of Military Posts in the Military Division of the Pacific.* California: Presidio of San Francisco Headquarters, 1879.

Mullin, Robert N. *The Boyhood of Billy the Kid.* Southwestern Studies Monograph No. 17. El Paso: Texas Western Press, 1967.

Nolan, Frederick. *The Lincoln County War: A Documentary History.* Norman: University of Oklahoma Press, 1992.

Otero, Miguel A. *The Real Billy the Kid: With New Light on the Lincoln County War.* New York: Rufus Rockwell Wilson, 1936.

Partridge, Eric. *The Penguin Dictionary of Historical Slang.* New York: Penguin Books, 1972.

Priestley, Lee. *Billy, the Kid: The Good Side of a Bad Man.* Las Cruces, New Mexico: Arroyo Press, 1989.

Santee, Ross. *Lost Pony Tracks.* New York: Charles Scribner's Sons, 1953.

Sloan, Richard E., ed. *History of Arizona.* 4 volumes. Phoenix: Record Publishing Co., 1930.

Stanley, F. *The Georgetown, New Mexico Story.* N.p., May 1963.

Tatum, Stephen. *Inventing Billy the Kid: Visions of the Outlaw in America, 1881-1981.* Albuquerque: University of New Mexico Press, 1982.

Utley, Robert M. *Billy the Kid: A Short and Violent Life.* Lincoln: University of Nebraska Press, 1989.

———. *Frontiersmen in Blue: The United States Army and the Indian, 1848-1865.* New York: Macmillan, 1967.

Walker, Henry P. and Don Bufkin. *Historical Atlas of Arizona.* Second edition. Norman: University of Oklahoma Press, 1986.

West, Elliott. *Growing Up With the Country: Childhood on the Far Western Frontier.* Albuquerque: University of New Mexico Press, 1989.

Williams, O. W. *Pioneer Surveyor, Frontier Lawyer: The Personal Narrative of O. W. Williams, 1877-1902.* Edited by S. D. Myres. El Paso: Texas Western College Press, 1966.

Woody, Clara T. and Milton L. Schwartz. *Globe, Arizona.* Tucson: Arizona Historical Society, 1977.

MANUSCRIPTS AND UNPUBLISHED MATERIALS

Anderson, Albie. "Billy the Kid Story." Attached to letter to Almer Blazer, October 31, 1931. Blazer Family Papers. Rio Grande Historical Collections. New Mexico State University, Las Cruces, New Mexico.

Conner, Anthony B., and Sister Mary J. Conner Swan. "Reminiscences of Southwestern New Mexico." Manuscript. Biographical File. Silver City Museum, Silver City, New Mexico.

Hartman, Louis. Complaint to Miles L. Wood, February 16, 1877. Photocopy. Author's files. (Original in National Archives, RG 93.)

Klasner, Lily. Papers. Brigham Young University, Provo, Utah.

Miliken, Marie Stevens. "Bonanza Bound: Isaac James Stevens and His Experiences as a Pioneer." Manuscript. Collection of Harvey H. Whitehill III.

Ming Family. Papers. Arizona Historical Society, Tucson.

Moulton, Ed. Biographical File. Silver City Museum, Silver City, New Mexico.

Naegle, Conrad Keeler. "The History of Silver City, New Mexico 1870-1886." Master's thesis, University of New Mexico, 1943.

Quinn, Leslie Wood. "Life Notes of M. L. Wood." Photocopy courtesy of the late Sally Quinn. Author's files.

Rothrock, George H. "The Life History of George H. Rothrock." Typescript. Rothrock Biographical File. Arizona Historical Foundation, Arizona State University Library, Tempe.

Truesdell, Chauncey O. Reminiscence, September 29, 1950. Typescript. Biographical File. Silver City Museum, Silver City, New Mexico.

Wood, Miles L. "Memories of Old Bonita." Photocopy courtesy of DuBois family papers and the late Sally Quinn. Author's files.

———. Reminiscences, 1911 and 1923. Photocopy courtesy of Irene Kennedy, DuBois family papers, and the late Sally Quinn. Author's files.

GOVERNMENT RECORDS

Arizona Department of Library, Archives and Public Records, Phoenix.

Arizona Census, 1874, 1876, 1878.

Pinal County Public Records.

Grant County Courthouse, Silver City, New Mexico.

Deed Books. County Clerk's Office.

National Archives.

Letters Received by the Office of Indian Affairs 1824-1881, Arizona Superintendency 1863-1880. M-234. Rolls 14-19.

Returns from Regular Army Cavalry Regiments 1833-1916. M-744. Roll 63.

Returns from U.S. Military Posts 1800-1916. M-617. Rolls 415 and 1265.

———. Record Group 93.

Letters and Telegrams Received, 1873-1905. Fort Grant, Arizona.

Post Returns and correspondence files.

———. Record Group 94.

Antrim, William. Pension affidavits.

Mackie, John R. Pension affidavits.

———. Record Group 159.

Biddle, James. Inspection Report and appendices.

———. Record Group 393.

Compton, Charles. Telegram to William Osborn. Telegram copy book, Fort Grant, Arizona, Vol. 35, Stock 9WZ 10:18C.

New Mexico State Records Center and Archives, Santa Fe.

District Court Docket Books. Grant County.

Marriage Record, 1863-1899. Santa Fe County Records.

Santa Fe County Courthouse, Santa Fe, New Mexico.

Book of Marriages.

University of Arizona Library, Tucson.

Government Documents.

Census, 1880. Grant County, New Mexico.

Special Collections.

    Great Registers for Pima County, 1874, 1876.

    Miscellaneous Pima County Territorial Records.

    Poll Lists of Electors, Tally Sheets, precinct of Camp Grant, 1874, 1876.

INTERVIEWS

Mullin, Robert N. Papers. J. Evetts Haley History Center, Midland, Texas.

    Curtis, Sidney H. and S. Ernest Pollack. Interviews by Robert Mullin, July 9, 1952.

    Stockbridge, Arthur. Interview by Robert N. Mullin, March 29, 1961.

    Truesdell, Chauncey O. Interview by Robert N. Mullin, January 9, 1952.

Museum of New Mexico, Santa Fe. WPA Files. History Library.

    Abraham, Louis. Interview by Frances E. Totty, November 23, 1937.

    Blair, Jim. Interview by Frances E. Totty, December 10, 1937.

    Clark, Dick. Interview by Frances E. Totty, November 15, 1937.

    Unnamed Silver City resident. Interview by Betty Reich, April 2, 1937.

Silver City Museum, Silver City, New Mexico. Historical Files.

    "Semi-Centennial Celebration." Typescript.

    Interviews by Helen Wheaton, September 3, 4, 1928.

        Abraham, Louis.

        Kilburn, Emma Whitehill.

        Whitehill, Harry.

Weddle, Jerry.

    DuBois, Dorothy and Henrietta. February, March, April, August 1987.

    Gray, Lucile. March 1988.

    Hughes, Jacqueline A. April 19, 1987.

    Kennedy, Irene F. February 17, 1987.

Whelan, Charles. Telephone conversation. March 19, 1987.

Zimmerman Library, University of New Mexico, Albuquerque. Pioneer's Foundation Recordings.

Snider, Agnes Meador. Interview by Louis Blachly. March 29, 1952.

Whitehill, Wayne. Interview by Louis Blachly. April 3, 1952.

LETTERS

Fulton, Maurice G. Papers. Special Collections, University of Arizona Library, Tucson.

Anderson, Leslie T. To Dear Lady [Florence Muzzy], May 26, 1874.

Conner, Anthony. To Maurice G. Fulton, April 29, June 26, 1932.

Gildea, Gus. To Maurice G. Fulton, January 16, 1929.

Upson, Ash. To Florence Muzzy, [after May 26, 1874].

Lincoln County Heritage Trust, Lincoln, New Mexico.

Bonney, William H. To General Lew Wallace, n.d. [March 13, 1879].

Mullin, Robert N. Papers. J. Evetts Haley History Center, Midland, Texas.

Abraham, Louis. To Maurice G. Fulton, April 22, 1932.

Silver City Museum, Silver City, New Mexico. John Swisshelm Biographical File.

Rhoades, Rendell. To Lena Shaw, January 23, 1872.

Weddle, Jerry.

Cox, Richard F. Military Reference Branch, Military Archives Division, National Archives, April 6, 1988.

Quinn, Kathy. February 1992.

Rasch, Philip J. August 22, 1992.

PHOTOGRAPHS

Museum of New Mexico, Santa Fe.

Negative #99054.

Silver City Museum, Silver City, New Mexico.

John Harlan Collection.
> Photograph #198 (c. 1878).
>
> Photograph #554 (c. 1875).
>
> Photographs of town c. 1872 - c. 1878.

MAPS

Arizona Historical Society, Tucson.
> Parts of Southeastern Arizona. Atlas Sheet No. 10. Department of Arizona. Lieutenant T. A. Touey, A. D. C., acting chief engineer.
>
> Sierra Bonita Ranch and Sulphur Springs Valley. 1880s.
>
> Southern Arizona. Late 1870s. Traced by Paul Riecker from map dated 1879, prepared under the direction of First Lieutenant Fred A. Smith, Adjutant, Twelfth Infantry.

Author's files.
> Arizona and New Mexico. c. 1882.
>
> Eckhoff, E. A., and P. Riecker. Territory of Arizona. 1880.
>
> Hamilton, Patrick. Territory of Arizona. 1884.
>
> Map of Arizona, 1878. Prepared specially for R. J. Hinton, *Hand-book to Arizona.*
>
> Territory of New Mexico. 1879. Department of the Interior, General Land Office. J. A. Williamson, Commissioner.

DuBois family files.
> Section map showing original landowners.

Grant County Courthouse, Silver City, New Mexico.
> Fraser, John R. Survey of Silver City, December 17, 1879. Deed Book 4.

National Archives and Records Administration. Geography and Map Division.
> Huggins, A. Z. Silver City, New Mexico. 1873.
>
> Proudfit, James K. Plat of the Town Site of Silver County, Grant County, New Mexico. November 19, 1872.

———. Record Group 75.
> Map 1135. Grant and Socorro Counties, New Mexico. c. 1888.

Map 166. New Mexico. 1873. Department of the Missouri.

———. Record Group 77.

Southern Part of Arizona. 1870.

Thomas, E. D. Military Reservation at Camp Grant, A. T. Miscellaneous Forts, Fort Grant No. 35.

———. Record Group 393.

Survey of Camp Grant Reservation and Surrounding Area. c. 1886. Department of Arizona No. 16.

New Mexico State Records Center and Archives, Santa Fe.

Morley's Map of New Mexico. 1873.

New Mexico Territory. 1876. Department of the Interior, General Land Office. J. A. Williamson, Commissioner.

Southwestern New Mexico. 1883.

Science and Engineering Library, University of New Mexico, Albuquerque.

Sanborn insurance maps. 1883, 1886, 1893, 1898.

Silver City Museum, Silver City, New Mexico.

Huggins, A. Z. 1873 Silver City diagram. Copy. (Original in Geography and Map Division, National Archives, Washington, D.C.)

Zimmerman Library, Center for Southwestern Studies, University of New Mexico.

Grant, A. A. Railroad and County Map of New Mexico. 1877.

Territory of New Mexico. 1879. Department of the Interior, General Land Office. J. A. Williamson, Commissioner.

OTHER SOURCES

Walking tours of Fort Grant and Bonita, February, March, April, August 1987, with Dorothy DuBois and Henrietta DuBois.

Index

Grant County, New Mexico, described, 2
Grant Creek, 33

H. M. Porter's General Merchandise Store, Silver City, 4
Hartman, Louis C., 36, 38
Hill, Tom, 46
Hog Ranch, Camp Grant, 33, 35-36
Hollinger, Mary Antrim, 1
Hooker, Henry C., 34
Hooker family, 35
Hoover, H. A., 58 n. 37
Hotel de Luna, Camp Grant, 32, 38, 39, 43, 61 n. 53
    photo of, 34
Hudson, Mary Stevens, 14-15
Hudson, Richard, 5, 14
Hudson's Hot Springs, New Mexico, 14
Hunt, James L. "Dobie," 44
Hunter, Thomas, 35

I. N. Cohen & Co., drygoods store, Silver City, 4
Irish, Lon, 56 n. 29
Isaac's Saloon, Globe City, 37

J. B. Bennett's Mercantile Store, Silver City, 5, 51 n. 7
Jack ("Former Resident"), 52 n. 12
Johnson, Nellie, 20, 56-57 n. 34
Justice, Richard, 11

Keays, Margaret. *See* Miller, Margaret Keays
Keystone Hotel, Silver City, 4, 51 n. 7
Kid. *See* McCarty, William Henry "Billy"
Kidd, William. *See* McCarty, William Henry "Billy"
Knight, Richard, 12, 18, 44
    meat market of, Silver City, 5, 18, 22
Knight, Sara Conner, 18, 44
Knight's Station, New Mexico, 44, 45
Knowler & Johnson's store, Bonita, 61 n. 53
Knox, T. R., 63 n. 57

McCune, Raymond, 56 n. 28
McDowell, Milton, 44
    store of, Camp Grant, 33, 35, 36, 61 n. 53
McFarland, Katie, 2
McFarland, Mrs. D. F., 2
McFarland, Reverend D. F., 2
McGary's bowling alley and dance hall, Silver City, 4, 6, 11
McIntosh, Charles, 23
McKittrick, George, brothel of, 33
McMillen, Charles, 36
McMillen's Camp, Arizona, 36
Main Street, Silver City, floods on, 51 n. 6
Maps,
    of Camp Grant, xix
    of southeastern Arizona and southwestern New Mexico, xvii
Market Street, Silver City, 12
Martin, Caleb, 35, 39
Mays, John, 7
Mays, Vincent, 7
Memory Lane Cemetery, Silver City, 56 n. 28
Miller, John A., 55 n. 28
Miller, Levi, 23
    photo of, 27
    blacksmith shop, photo of, 29
Miller, Margaret Keays, 23
    photo of, 33
Mimms, Old Man, 50 n. 4
Ming, Daniel H., 62 n. 56
Mining Life (Silver City), 9
Moore, Thomas, murder of, 59-60 n. 48
Morrill, J. B., store, Silver City, 4
Mose (member of Banditti), 46
Moulton, Ed, 23, 53 n. 16
    friend of Antrim family, 2, 6, 45, 46, 50 n. 4, 58 n. 38
    sawmill of, Bear Mountain, 29
Murphey, John, 43

Nevada Hotel, Silver City, 51 n. 7

Van Wagenen, Jennie Ramsdell. *See* Ramsdell, Jennie
Varley, Tom, 41
Village Arabs, 9, 11
    crimes of, 12, 13-14, 20, 57 n. 35
    minstrel shows in Silver City, 12-13
    schooling of, 16

Wagner, P., Silver City barber, 4
Ward's Hall, Silver City, 6
Webb, Abel L., 24
Webster, Dr. J., 11
Whelan, Charles, 62 n. 55
Whelan, William, 34, 62 n. 55
Whitehill family, 18, 60 n. 50
Whitehill, Con, photo of, 20
Whitehill, Emma, xiv, 11, 12, 21, 23
    photo of, 20
Whitehill, Harriet, 26-27
Whitehill, Harry, as contemporary of Billy McCarty, xiv, xv, 7,
    11, 12, 13, 23, 24, 31
    photo of, 20
Whitehill, Harvey H., and crimes of Billy McCarty, 24-30, 45-47
    described, 23
Whitehill, Hattie, photo of, 20
Whitehill, Josie, photo of, 20
Whitehill, Olive, 19
    photo of, 20
Whitehill, Wayne, as contemporary of Billy McCarty, 7, 19, 21,
    23, 53 n. 18
    harassment of Charlie Sun, 20
    photo of, 20
Wichita, Kansas, 1
Wilson, William, assault by Joe Dyer, 11
Wilson, William, in Lincoln County War, 53 n. 16
Wood, Miles L., xv, 35
    as Camp Grant justice of the peace, 38, 39, 40, 41, 42-43
    as proprietor of Hotel de Luna, 32, 61 n. 53
    photo of, 37

Photographic Credits

Photograph on cover courtesy of Lincoln County Heritage Trust, Upham Collection

Handwriting on cover from a letter from William H. Bonney to General Lew Wallace, courtesy of Lincoln County Heritage Trust, Wallace Collection.

Photograph on p. 3 courtesy of Special Collections, University of Arizona Library, Tucson

Photograph on p. 4 courtesy of Leon C. Metz

Photograph on p. 5 courtesy of Jerry Weddle

Photographs on pp. 8 and 15 are loaned by Leah Lockart, great-granddaughter of David Abraham

Photographs on pp. 9 and 20 courtesy of Denver Public Library, Western History Department

Photographs on pp. 10 and 16 courtesy of Kelly Truesdell

Photograph on p. 21 courtesy of Fred E. Prevost, Jr.

Photograph on p. 25 courtesy of Harvel H. Cosper

Photograph on p. 27 from Helen Haines, *History of New Mexico . . .*

Photographs on pp. 28 and 32 courtesy of the Silver City Museum, Silver City, New Mexico

Photograph on p. 29 courtesy of the John Harlan Collection, Silver City Museum

Photograph on p. 33 courtesy of Jean Uhli

Photographs on pp. 34 and 37 courtesy of Irene Hancock Kennedy

Photograph on p. 41 courtesy of the private collection of C. Robert Bigando

The Arizona Historical Society, 1993

Michael F. Weber, executive director
Buck Clark, president
Bruce J. Dinges, director of publications

The Publications Committee

Patricia Davis Brandt, chair
Bruce J. Dinges
L. Boyd Finch
John S. Goff
Mary Hays
Salvador Martinez
James E. Officer
Hank Oyama
Richard Salvatierra
Lillian Theobald

This book was set in 11/14 Stone Serif on a Macintosh
Quadra 700. It was printed by Arizona Lithographers of Tucson,
and bound by Roswell Bookbinding of Phoenix.

Designed by John Meyer.